Article on
Gissing
Conrad,
Strindberg

Voices of To-morrow

BY EDWIN BJÖRKMAN

GLEAMS
IS THERE ANYTHING NEW UNDER THE SUN?
VOICES OF TO-MORROW

Mr. Björkman is the authorized translator of the Plays of August Strindberg now being published by Charles Scribner's Sons.

VOICES OF TO-MORROW: CRITICAL STUDIES OF THE NEW SPIRIT IN LITERATURE

Edwin Björkman

MITCHELL KENNERLEY
New York and London
MCMXIII

Copyright 1913 by Mitchell Kennerley

Dear M. K.:

What makes me dedicate this book to you is neither the faith you showed in my work when others viewed it with complete indifference, nor your generous and faithful friendship, often more mindful of my interests than of your own, but the fact that you seem to me one of those foresighted few who have come to realize that "success in business" is a meaningless term unless used as a symbolical equivalent for "service rendered."

March, 1913.

Since its first appearance in "The Forum," the Strindberg study has been doubled in length and almost wholly rewritten. In its new form it includes a few paragraphs taken from my introduction to Strindberg's "There are Crimes and Crimes." The second Herrick study is new. The rest of the articles contained in this volume have previously appeared in "The American Review of Reviews," "The Bookman," "The New York Call," "The New York Times," and "The Forum." For permission to reprint them I am beholden to the editors of those publications. The Gissing study was written in 1904. All the others have been produced during the last four years. None of them pretends to be more than suggestive. Demands from without have to a certain extent compelled the choice of subjects, and so it happens, to my great regret, that, in this volume again, German thought and literature remain unrepresented.

CONTENTS

AUGUST STRINDBERG	11
1 His Life	11
2 His Work	41
3 His Spirit	85
4 Bibliographical	117
BJÖRNSTJERNE BJÖRNSON	121
Poet, Politician, Prophet	121
THE STORY OF SELMA LAGERLÖF	139
THE NEW MYSTICISM	154
1 Its Prophet: Francis Grierson	154
2 Its Poet: Maurice Maeterlinck	186
3 Its Philosopher: Henri Bergson	205
GRAAL KNIGHTS OF MODERN LETTERS	224
1 George Gissing	224
2 Joseph Conrad	240
TWO STUDIES OF ROBERT HERRICK	260
THE GREATER EDITH WHARTON	290
MAN'S BEGINNING AND END	305

AUGUST STRINDBERG

I

His Life

"PEOPLE are sometimes blamed for speaking of themselves," says Anatole France, "and yet it is the subject which they treat of best." August Strindberg asserted with his usual directness, that the only fiction really worth while is the one that deals unreservedly with the author's own self.

It is doubtful whether the world ever knew an artist who was more consistently and unshrinkingly personal in his choice of material. At the same time, however, I doubt whether any one was ever more impersonal in his treatment of such material. "In the last analysis," writes a competent Swedish critic, "he was always looking at himself with the eyes of a stranger."

But even in the case of one whose art was thus inextricably mixed with his life, I maintain that his work, if possessed of genuine greatness, must be intelligible without reference to anything lying outside its own frame. And I do not for a moment believe that any amount of personal detail can explain genius—much less explain it *away*. In giving an outline of certain influences and experiences known to have played the part of a refracting medium to the essential spirit of Strindberg's genius, I wish only to provide an easier approach to the understanding of his work, where alone may be found that true color of his soul which is likely to make his name live in the future.

The *leit motif* of his childhood was built out of two jarring notes: misunderstanding and isolation. He was an unwelcome child. Throughout life he remained more or less unwelcome, isolated and misunderstood. And if at times we find in his work a note of bitterness bordering on hatred, we must recall not only the sad beginnings, but also the subsequent stress and struggle through which he had to force his way to the point where he stood at the time of his death—tardily recognized as the greatest living writer in the Scandinavian North and one of the greatest in the whole world.

Strindberg's father was a shopkeeper who had gone bankrupt a short time before the child was born, and who had to begin life all over again as a steamship agent. The boy's mother was a barmaid who had brought three children into the world before her relation to their father was legitimized by marriage. And a couple of months after the wedding August was born. That was in January, 1849.

The family was living in Stockholm, the gay capital of Sweden, but its members had less contact with the rest of the world than if they had been stranded in a desert. The father turned with almost monomaniacal devotion to the task of building up a secure livelihood for himself and those depending on him. The mother was narrowly religious and wholly preoccupied with the cares of a constantly growing brood. The home was, for years, of the poorest—and as child after child was added to the flock, its three rooms had finally to house eleven persons: the parents, seven children, and two servants.

The boy's first remembered sensations, as recorded by himself, were fear and hunger—and of those two, fear predominated. Thus we may guess why so often in later life his indomitable courage seemed tinged with desperation. Timid and shy, morbidly sensitive, craving love and justice with equal passion where both seemed denied him, he became from the very start what he often called himself—one of life's scapegoats. At the age of eight he dreamt of taking his own life because he had been unjustly accused and then tormented into falsely acknowledging himself guilty of the charge. And what hurt him more than the unmerited punishment was the doubting of his word. No other incident in his life seems to have struck such deep roots in his mind as this one, sowing within him a distrust not only of his fellow men, but of life itself and what lies behind it, that he was never able to overcome. Plain echoes of that childish experience are to be heard in one work after another.

His mother's religiosity was of the egoistical kind that refers only to the salvation of the individual soul. The father, being more intellectual, was more passive in his attitude, but hardly broader in his faith. The boy, on the other hand, seems from the first to have fermented with an emotion which, while it sought outlet in religious forms, was largely social in its trend. Here again we find a chasm yawning between the boy and his surroundings that helped to swing him toward an extreme of materialistic scepticism before he could find true expression for one of the fundamental tendencies in his nature. And the same influence went far, I think, to pull him back time and again into a morbid jealousy on behalf of his own personality.

When he was thirteen, his mother died, and he mourned not so much her death as the final loss of that tender sympathy which his soul hungered for, but which all his longings had never been able to draw from her. Perhaps it was this first fatal disappointment which doomed him to repeated disillusionment in his subsequent intercourse with the other sex. He himself has said somewhere that he could never tell whether he was looking to women for a mother's love or that of a mistress.

Before a year had passed, he was given a stepmother—and once more his soul received a shock never to be forgotten. He tried to like her and make himself liked. In both efforts he failed conspicuously. And the only result was increased estrangement between himself and his father. Thus everything combined to throw him back upon himself, and to further that habit of intense introspection which was to form such a characteristic trait of his art. The one consoling circumstance of those crucial years from thirteen to eighteen was that the financial position of the household became very much improved, so that the boy, after a couple of unhappy educational experiences, could attend a good private school and hope for a university course. But when at last, at the age of eighteen, he departed for the ancient university in the little town of Upsala—Sweden's Oxford—his total means consisted of eighty *kronor* (about $22) which he had earned for himself by tutoring. From his father he received nothing but a handful of cigars and the advice to "look out for himself."

During the greater part of his stay at the university he was wretchedly poor. He did not even have money enough to buy wood for the heating of the bare garret where he lived. Sometimes he borrowed a sackful from some more fortunate comrade, carrying it home on his own back, and sometimes he stayed in bed for days to keep warm.

His first term was almost lost because he had no books and no money to buy any. But worse than all this was the rebellion inspired within him by the futility of the whole academical system. Once he broke away in despair and began to teach in one of the public schools at Stockholm. He was assigned to the lowest grade, and realized quickly that he had exchanged one hell for another. Like *The Lieutenant* in "The Dream Play," he imagined himself condemned to start the whole dreary routine over again, not as a teacher, but as one of the pupils—bored, scolded and snubbed.

It is of no use here to talk of lacking flexibility or adaptability. Young Strindberg's story is that of numerous other men of genius. They are all fitted for some particular task—and until they find that task they are helpless. Rousseau, Balzac, Wagner, Ibsen, Shaw are among those that may be mentioned in illustration. And it is to be noted that during the period in question Strindberg was firmly convinced of his own inability to write. He had tried, and —"nothing would come." His family regarded him as a good-for-nothing. And he himself was, on the whole, fearful that their judgment might prove correct.

We can then imagine his surprise and rapture, when, during that temporary absence from the university, he discovered that, after all, the gift of poetical creation was his. It was as if some frozen fountain had thawed out and sent a flood of inspiration through his whole being. In a couple of months (in 1869) he produced several comedies and a five-act tragedy in verse on a classical theme. This he named "Hermione," and to this day it remains distinctly readable. A one-act verse play was accepted and played at the Royal Theatre. Strindberg was then twenty-one. A little later (1871) another small play, "The Outcast"—a historical prose study undoubtedly suggested by Björnson's "Between the Battles"—won him the attention of King

Charles XV and a stipend from the monarch's private purse.

While this spell of sunshine lasted, he returned to the university to make another vain attempt at winning a degree. He read prodigiously—and some of his reading actually overlapped the courses prescribed by the curriculum. But as a rule his mind followed its own impulses. The keynote of his entire existence at the time was an intense intellectual curiosity. "To study everything, to know everything, was a mania with me," he said of himself later. That mania remained typical of his mental attitude throughout all the vicissitudes of his life. And I think that, more than once, it proved the saving factor when he found himself brought to the very brink of irremediable disaster. Nor was there ever anything superficial about this insatiable curiosity. Whether searching his own soul or observing surrounding nature, he must needs go to the bottom of things. Thus I found not long ago that he had examined the botanical text books in six different languages merely to clear up some obscure point. And the mercilessness of his introspection is splendidly illustrated by a passage in which he describes a character who is none but himself in slight disguise: "Falk was a vivisector who experimented on his own soul, always going around with open wounds, until he gave his life for the sake of knowledge."

During his second stay at the university he made three spiritual acquaintances which became largely determining for his future development. They were the Danish philosopher Kierkegaard's "Either—Or," which made him for ever a champion of the ethical, as juxtaposed to the esthetical, life conception; Buckle's "History of Civilization in England," which revealed to him the relativity of truth and the rooting of all ideas in material conditions; and, finally, Eduard von Hartmann's "Philosophy of the Unconscious," which introduced him to the gospel of pessimism, the acceptance of life as an inevitable and, perhaps, meaningless evil. Afterwards Strindberg travelled many strange paths and worshipped at many new shrines, but he remained always faithful in spirit to those earlier guides; and to the last he proclaimed in his books and plays that art and knowledge must be subservient to life, and that life itself must be lived as we know best, chiefly because we are part of it and cannot escape from its promptings.

He wrote, too, during that period, but destroyed everything without having made an attempt to get it played or published. Two historical five-act tragedies were among the products sacrificed to his growing power of self-criticism. With the death of the king in 1872, his stipend ceased and distress returned. Unable to study, unable to write, unable to do anything but paint—in which art he also reached considerable proficiency without ever having studied it in prescribed fashion—he feared that he was losing his mind. On one occasion comrades had to watch at his bed for several nights while every available candle was kept burning to shield him from the horrors lurking in the darkness. And once the future author of "Inferno," who was to drift as close to the border-line between the rational and the irrational as any one may dare without fatal results, actually wrote to a private sanitarium for advice.

In the end he gave up the vain struggle for academical preferment and returned to Stockholm. A lucky chance took him out to one of the innumerable islands that make the inlet to Stockholm one of the most beautiful in the world. There, during two quietly happy summer months, he wrote his first masterpiece, "Master Olof," a historical prose drama grouped around the Luther of the Swedish Reformation. Forty years have passed since Strindberg, then only twenty-three years old, completed that work. Forty years of shifting literary fashions have failed to sap its strength or dim its charm. But while it still seems great to-day, even when compared with the epoch-making works of universal literature, it stood unique in Swedish literature at the time of its completion—a landmark proclaiming the inception of a new era.

But it was rejected—scornfully and sneeringly rejected—by the literary arbiters of the Royal Theatre, then the only stage available for the production of such a work. No publisher could be found for it. Not until five years later was it placed before the public in book form, and then in altered shape, after its author had rewritten it five times in compliance with the edict of the critics that verse alone was suitable to the historical drama—an opinion voiced about the same time by Edmund Gosse in regard to Ibsen's "Emperor and Galilean." The first stage performance of "Master Olof" did not occur until 1880, and then on one of the privately managed stages that had begun to spring up in the capital.

For a time the reception accorded his first authentical work of genius seemed to rob Strindberg of the very desire to write. His struggle for mere existence became more trying than ever. At last, after having failed as an actor and as a hack writer for various newspapers, he obtained a position in the National Library. There he spent his time in studying Chinese and writing monographs on the relations between China and Sweden in the eighteenth century. One of these efforts was even read before the French Institute and brought him a medal from the Russian Geographical Society.

He was twenty-six, and the arch-rebel within him appeared to have received a quietus for ever, when he met the woman who was to exercise an influence on his fate comparable to that first impression of the world's blind injustice which had burned itself so ineradicably into the boy's consciousness. She was another man's wife. Of the vicissitudinous courtship that ensued I shall not speak here. In the end a divorce left the woman free to marry the man who had already been her lover for some time. Throughout that transitory period, as well as afterwards, the passing and the coming husband seem to have regarded each other not only without ill-will, but with real friendship. In the whole matter inhered, however, an ambiguity that must have hurt Strindberg to the quick. For the man to whose "marital ventures" jeering references have so often been made was above everything else *clean* in all his instincts. And that he had to reach his dreamed happiness through what the world calls a scandal was sure to call forth a reaction sooner or later.

But happiness he had for a time—the first genuine happiness of his life. And under that stimulus he began to write again: first a series of short stories, and then a novel, "The Red Room." This was his second masterpiece. It established his reputation as a writer, though his own countrymen did their best to overlook the book. In the end it won its way largely through the recognition bestowed on it by critics in the other Scandinavian countries. During the

AUGUST STRINDBERG

next few years Strindberg's literary productivity was tremendous. But I shall here speak of only one more work from that period—the first of the two short-story volumes named "Marriage." He wrote it in Switzerland, whither he had withdrawn to give himself wholly to his art. The impetus to it came unmistakably from Ibsen's "A Doll's House," against which Strindberg reacted antipathetically from the first. His immediate object was merely to present modern marriage as he saw it—based not on "ideal demands," but on economical conditions. But as usual he spoke what he held to be the truth with such force that evasion became impossible.

Criminal proceedings were instituted, not against Strindberg, but against his publisher, and not for "immorality" but for—sacrilegious treatment of the established religion. By hurrying home, Strindberg succeeded in turning the fire on himself. While the proceedings lasted, the whole country was literally split in twain over the issues involved. It was the old and the new fighting for supremacy. The jury at last brought in a verdict of "not guilty," and the author was acclaimed with a fervor rarely if ever displayed toward a literary man in Sweden. He was thereafter the acknowledged leader of a band of radical poets and artists who called themselves "Young Sweden." But in the midst of the feasting and shouting, the object of all that enthusiasm whispered to himself: "Yes, you cheer me to-day, and to-morrow you will be hissing me." And the main impression retained by his mind was not of the joyous tumult caused by his acquittal, but of the humiliation that had led up to it—for he felt that his aim had been unmistakably pure.

That was in 1884. His marriage lasted seven years longer, but with every passing year the relationship between him and his wife grew more painful. Time and again he tried to break the bond, and as often he returned, drawn back partly by lingering love, and partly by that "link" which held him most powerfully—the children. And not only love for wife and children, but his entire natural bent, made it hard for him to seek relief from a burden become unbearable. For though he had won another man's wife, and though he was to marry twice again, he was instinctively and passionately monogamous. And one of the main tragedies of his all too tragic life was his inability to realize the ideal of two souls walking side by side through life, bound together by a love that had in it no touch of impurity.

Omniscience would be needed to proclaim the exact degree of responsibility attaching to the man and the woman in that marriage. The hellish tortures which it inflicted on both parties to it have been pictured by Strindberg in his autobiographical novel, "A Fool's Confession," with a minute exactness and a psychological penetration that have probably never been surpassed. Some of the charges and insinuations contained in that remarkable book may be exaggerated, or even imagined, but to one knowing the man, his uncanny faculty for observation, and his irresistible tendency to record the truth in spite of himself, the conclusion seems inevitable that, on the whole, the picture of marital life presented in the book is correct. Where Strindberg made his mistake was in letting himself be tempted by his just grievances into mistaking the specimen for the species, the individual for the type. When he thought himself arraigning *woman,* his charges were in reality directed against *a* woman—his wife. And his later pictures of married life showed this form of human relationship not as it must be and always is, but as it may be and often becomes. Personally I believe that he never wrote a line that did not contain something of truth in it. But I believe also that frequently—and especially during the period in question—he mistook *a* truth for *the* truth.

While the final catastrophe was still impending, he wrote some of his most wonderful dramatic works—the three-act modern tragedy named "The Father," and his first group of iconoclastic one-act plays, with "Miss Julia" and "Creditors" preceding and surpassing all the rest. During a stay at Berlin, while he was still striving to recover from the shock imparted to his whole system by the divorce from his first wife, he met and courted a sympathetic German woman, a writer also, whose tastes seemed congenial to his own. This second experiment lasted only a few years. It was not so violently unhappy as the first one, but the experiences it implied helped undoubtedly to bring on the crisis which finally overtook Strindberg at the age of forty-five—an age that almost always plays a significant part in the lives of greatly gifted men—and which served to wipe several years out of his existence as an artistic creator.

At all times, from his earliest youth to the day of his death, he was keenly interested in every aspect of life not only as an artist but as a thinker. He studied every branch of modern science from astronomy to sociology. Nature was to him always a book which he read with never-failing fascination. The comments of other men on that book were also of interest to him, but at no time was he inclined to accept them unchallenged. Some day the world will know what a treasure trove of suggestive ideas lies hidden among Strindberg's scientific and philosophical speculations, even when these appear most fantastic. Not that I believe him always to have been in the right, but I think that, in his criticism of modern science, however uncharitable it be in form, he was always on the track of some truth still hidden from the patient plodders in the field involved.

From an early period, when a physician's calling was in his mind and actually led him into the dissecting room and the laboratory, he entertained a passionate fondness for chemistry and its problems. During the time of which I am now speaking those problems engrossed his mind completely.

AUGUST STRINDBERG

The will-o'-the-wisp pursued most ardently was the transmutability of elements hitherto supposed to be stable and irreducible. Back of that dream lay the older one of *making gold,* and it was with this that Strindberg's overwrought fancy became more and more preoccupied. But not for the sake of gain. What he sought, then as always, was truth —and it is as a seeker after truth, after spiritual treasures, that Strindberg should be fixed in our minds.

His strange search at Paris in the middle nineties brought him what he looked for, but not exactly in the form that he had expected. For he found not ordinary gold but—the mystic faith of Swedenborg. Through this faith he won his way once more to health and strength and spiritual balance and creative power. But ere he reached that far, he nearly sacrificed both life and reason. There is another autobiographical work, "Inferno," in which he told of his travels through the nethermost regions of despair and delusion. In all the world's literature there is not another book quite its equal. It is a document that must enter as one of the foundation stones of our coming understanding of the human mind.

Returning to Sweden in the summer of 1896, Strindberg actually spent a couple of months in a private sanitarium kept by an old friend. A year later he began to write again—first of all the volumes embodying the mental crisis just completed. And then, while all the world was still thinking him lost for ever, there ensued a period of such miraculously creative activity that soon its results eclipsed all his earlier achievements. Plays, modern and historical, realistic and symbolistic; novels and stories; pamphlets of critical, scientific and political bearing; verse and prose; works of playful fancy and others filled with the deepest pathos—a whole literature in short, with all its attendant subdivisions, seemed to pour forth in unbroken stream from his fertile brain.

Of his private life during the final period it is hardly necessary to speak. Even when his fame rose into higher and higher flood tide, there came days of disappointment and sorrow. Too often his efforts—even the best—were met with a lack of understanding, or a premeditated misconstruction, that tempted the berserker nature within him into outbursts like those contained in certain chapters of his last novel, "Black Flags," or in the pamphlet entitled "Speeches to the Swedish Nation." But in the main the tenor of his existence had become determined, and what happened for good or bad might disturb but not alter his general trend. There was a third marriage—a final search for the dreamed ideal. It was the briefest and least turbulent of his marital episodes. Then the solitude closed in around him again—the solitude in the midst of a multitude which he pictured so touchingly in "Alone." It was no longer quite unwelcome. He might have been unreservedly happy but for one lack—that of children, *his* children. Not that he ever lost track of any one of them—there being five in all sprung from the three marriages—but he wanted them always around him.

Toward those children, even more than toward their mothers, his heart went out in periods of estrangement and impending separation. To surrender them brought him deeper pain than any other loss. And yet he never tried to keep them wholly to himself, because he felt so strongly that children belong primarily to the mother for their own sake. It was fear of the mother's unworthiness as mother that raised his anger to a greater degree of fierceness than anything else. For though he had never received from his own mother the fullness of love he craved, he showed for his offspring a tenderness and a devotion such as commonly the mother alone is held capable of. He might truly be named the poet of fatherhood—and it must be held thoroughly characteristic that he named his most poignant tragedy "The Father," and not "The Husband."

It is frequently asserted nowadays, that

AUGUST STRINDBERG 37

the father's love for the child is more or less acquired, more or less reasoned, while that of the mother is instinctive and spontaneous. Against this view Strindberg carried on incessant warfare. In his eye the child appeared as strongly and as inevitably tied to one parent as to the other. And beneath this tie he saw the individual's craving for continued existence in the child. One of the main issues in that duel of the sexes which forms such a conspicuous theme of his art is the struggle of each parent to impress his or her nature on the child, to the exclusion of the other one's. What his work might have been, if fate had granted him undisturbed enjoyment of that triple happiness which he repeatedly pictured in such glowing colors—the happiness of home and wife and children—no amount of speculation can reveal.

In January, 1912, all Sweden and much of Europe celebrated Strindberg's sixty-third birthday anniversary—his arrival at that "great climacteric" which, like the ancient Greeks, he regarded as the gateway to old age. He was far from well at the time and took no part in the festivities arranged in his honor except by appearing for a few minutes at his window while a procession of workmen filed past with their banners and torchlights.

Not long afterwards the reports about his condition became more serious, and at last it was found that he had long been suffering from cancer of the stomach. Though in great pain much of the time, he remained to the last faithful to his Horatian motto: *Speravit infestis*—which may be translated as "hopeful in adversity."

His death occurred on May 14, 1912. On the day before the last he called for his Bible, which he always kept within easy reach. Placing his hand on it, he said quietly: "Everything personal is now wiped out. I have settled with life. My balance has been struck. This book alone is right." A few moments later he added: "Now I have spoken my last words; now I'll say no more." And from that moment until the end came, he lay so still and silent that the children gathered about his bed could not tell whether he was conscious or not.

As we see the real man Strindberg, with his life cleared of foolish legends and hostile interpretations, he was neither an ogre nor a sphinx, but, on the whole, a very simple human being. Simple he was always in his tastes, simple and direct in his likes and dislikes, in his violent hatreds and strong affections. Above all else he worshipped the three things which never appealed to Ibsen: music, flowers and children.

At heart he was, I think, an incurable sentimentalist—and like all true sentimentalists he was, on the surface, all contradiction, all conflict, all vain struggle to reach a point of equilibrium where the million paradoxes of life should become resolved into a single absolute truth. His reason was clearer and more comprehensive than that of most men; yet it was insufficient for the adequate control of the emotional pressure from within. His reason furnished a channel for his every expression. It was the main outlet of all his activity as man and artist. Where another man might have been stirred into murder, he was moved into merciless analysis of his own and other people's soul states. But his motives were always rooted below his head, so to speak. In this fact lies probably the explanation why he became an artist rather than a philosopher, and why he showed such lack of restraint in his attacks on men and things that would not square with the demands of his own spirit.

To sum him up in the fewest possible number of words, I wish once more to quote Anatole France, who wrote of Benjamin Constant what might as well have been written of Strindberg: "We may judge this man severely, but there is one greatness we cannot deny him: he was very unhappy, and that is not the lot of a mean soul."

II

HIS WORK

TURNING from the man to what he achieved, we meet first of all with evidence of a startling and almost limitless manysidedness. Since the days of Goethe the world has not known a creative mind so catholic in its interests, or a pen so adaptable to every literary form. He touched every field of human thought—astronomy, mineralogy, chemistry, botany, zoology, biology, psychology, sociology, economy, history, philology, philosophy, ethics, esthetics —and rarely without notable results. To the field more particularly his own he contributed with almost equal success as poet, novelist, essayist and playwright.

Nor was his passion to embrace all life within a single consciousness restricted to a single mode of expression—by means of the written word. I have already mentioned his noteworthy excursions into painting, twice revealed to his astonished countrymen by interesting exhibitions (and by the fact that in the little Parisian *crêmerie* which has been reproduced with photographic exactness in "There Are Crimes and Crimes," his paintings were much treasured but his writings wholly unknown). He was also a musician of fine discernment, and some of the music that figures so largely in his plays was arranged, or even composed, by himself. And during the final years of his life, while staking all he had on a theatrical experiment for the exclusive production of his own plays, he showed himself a stage director of great ability and daring ingenuity.

As a writer he impresses us not only by the variety but also by the amount of his production. The definite Swedish edition of his collected works will contain from fifty to sixty volumes—or something like six million words. If somebody tried to read them

AUGUST STRINDBERG 43

aloud, giving to the task eight hours a day, it would take him more than two years to finish those volumes. But even such figures as these fail to bring home the full extent of his achievement. A classified summary of his works, some of which are only now being published for the first time, will go farther in this direction. This is what such a list has to offer us:

Fifty-six plays, varying in length from a single scene like "The Stronger" to the mighty trilogy named "Toward Damascus;" nineteen volumes of novels and stories; eleven volumes of autobiographical fiction; three volumes of verse; sixteen volumes of historical and scientific writings; seventeen collections of essays, criticism, notes, etc.

Much supercilious and some warranted criticism has been evoked by his ventures outside his own domain as a poet in the wider meaning of the term: as a writer of creative, imaginative literature. Final judgment must lie with the future, of course, and the audacity of all his thinking, whether embodied in artistic or non-artistic form, will tend still further to make that future a distant one. For the present this much may be safely asserted: that his mind never dealt with any line of human knowledge without uncovering new and startling vistas.

As a historian he compelled imitation even where he failed to win approval. His greatest work of this kind, "The Swedish People in War and Peace," was, in spite of admitted shortcomings, distinctly pathbreaking both in character and effect. To-day this work is, next to the Bible, the one most read among the Swedes in the United States. As a keen-eyed and tenderly sympathetic observer of nature and of all life subordinate to that of man, he has not often been excelled. His more pretentious efforts at scientific thinking and writing were undoubtedly marred by the venturesomeness of a mind accustomed to rely equally on intuition and on intellect for its conclusions. But even here some of his more daring suggestions have already been overtaken by the more slowly advancing forces of organized knowledge. Thus, to mention only one instance, the charming little essay called "The Intellect of Animals and Plants" may have seemed purely fantastic at the time of its publication in 1888. To-day it stands recognized as a definite herald of ideas since then scientifically formulated by men like Sir Francis Darwin. And at the same time one may well ask whether it did not furnish Maeterlinck with suggestions for his "The Intelligence of the Flowers," which it closely foreshadows.

Regarding Strindberg primarily as an imaginatively creative writer, we find his career as such falling into three sharply defined periods. The first of these lasted from 1868 to 1885; the second, from 1886 to 1894; the third, from 1897 to his death. Between the second and the third periods occurred that interregnum of absolute unproductivity, of which I have already spoken and to which I shall again refer.

For purposes of convenience, rather than with any claim at positive definition, those periods may be designated as: 1) the romantic; 2) the naturalistic; 3) the symbolistic. Of course, a tendency to naturalistic presentation of external facts characterized his work almost from the start, and it continued to assert itself even in the most mystical products of his final period. He was always a realist in the finest sense of that term—one insisting that art must cling closely to life as actually lived and stand firmly on this ground even when reaching most daringly into still unconquered realms of being. But on the other hand, there was always a touch of mysticism, of yearning idealism, of instinctive out-reaching for the life still to come, even in such characteristic works of the middle period as "The Father" and "Creditors." It represented a strain of feeling and thought nearly inseparable from the Scandinavian temperament.

Of the first period, beginning with his initial gropings in the world of poetry, and coming to an end, in 1885, with the completion of the four short stories published collectively as "Real Utopias," I have dared to speak as romantic chiefly because sentiment still holds almost equal sway with logic in the work belonging to it. Strindberg has generally been described as a pupil of Zola. As a fact, he was not familiar with the work of the great French novelist when he established his own style and outlook in "The Red Room." As a boy and young man, he read whatever the world-literature had to offer him of lasting value. Goethe, Schiller and the Dane Oehlenschläger were among his earliest ideals. A little later he studied Dante and Shakespeare—in their native tongues—and against both he reacted rather unsympathetically. The main reason was that he found them established as idols which one had to worship at the penalty of being declared lacking in taste and knowledge. He said in one of his autobiographical novels that, as he had found it much less dangerous to attack Christ than

Shakespeare, he had chosen the latter to prove his critical fearlessness. Toward the end of his life he published a series of comments on the principal Shakespeare dramas which proved him at once a discriminating student and an ardent lover of England's Bard.

But his chief artistic forbears were Hugo, Dickens, the brothers de Goncourt, and Mark Twain. To the Englishman and the two Frenchmen he confessed his indebtedness repeatedly, and he maintained with his usual strenuousness that Dickens must be counted among those who had done most to bring modern poetry back to real life. The influence exercised on him by the great American humorist remained long unrecognized, but of late it has been pointed out by several Swedish critics. And it is also recalled that one of his first literary efforts took the form of a series of translations including some of Mark Twain's most characteristic work. The stimulus which his ever susceptible fancy received from still another American writer did not become revealed until a few months after his death. Then the Swedish poet and novelist Ola Hansson published a number of letters divulging the fact that Strindberg had been eagerly reading some of Edgar Allan Poe's tales just before he produced such plays as "Creditors," "Pariah," and "Simoom," and the novels "Chandalah" and "At the Edge of the Sea." Of the inspiration which, at a much later time, he drew from Maeterlinck and other mystical writers, I shall speak further on.

The transition from the first to the second period caused no interruption in his creative activity. Evidence that some kind of border line was crossed about 1885 must be drawn from within the works then produced. But the moment we compare the preface of the first part of "Marriage," dating from 1884, with that of the second part, written in 1886, we perceive that something of moment must have happened in the meantime. Of course, the real events took place in

Strindberg's own mind. But the principal external facts connected with those inner changes were the confiscation of the first part of "Marriage" and the beginnings of his marital unhappiness.

We know now, through the recently published reminiscences of an unbiased and clear-eyed friend (Hélène Welinder: Strindberg in Switzerland: *Ord och Bild,* Stockholm, September, 1912), that when, during the summer of 1884, Strindberg and Siri von Essen celebrated their seventh wedding anniversary, they were still conscious of a deep happiness in their common life. And we know also from the same source that shortly afterwards the wife's growing impatience with a merely domestic career began to break into open flame, while the husband seemed to regard the very idea of her reappearance on the stage with a scorn and a disgust that he had not evidenced during the first years of their marriage. It was this growing tension between two opposed wills that nursed the subsequent estrangement of their spirits, until a burning love turned into burning hatred.

His altered attitude toward womanhood is the first thing that makes itself felt in the second of the two prefaces already referred to. But back of it we suspect the presence of changes reaching much farther down into the writer's conception of life. The man who wrote the first part of "Marriage" and "Real Utopias" was, on the whole, well content with his world. The author of the second part of "Marriage" and of "The Father" strikes us, on the other hand, as a man doubting the very possibility of happiness as a human state.

I deem it highly regrettable that for many years hardly any works by Strindberg except those dating from his middle period became known in the English-speaking countries. For in many respects I cannot but think that period abnormal—representing a deviation from his true line of development. During those years between 1885 and 1894, the nature of Strindberg, which was no whit less capable of love and faith than of hatred and doubt, became sadly warped. All the world lay wrapt in grey mist. Woman, once angelic, turned into a devil incarnate. Life was seen as war to the hilt—and love was the worst form this war could assume.

To me it seems quite logical that this period, and no other, should see Strindberg turn from his former social outlook to a temporary acceptance of Nietzsche's ultra-individualistic superman theories. It is the works from this period that have brought him the name of a misogynist and the reputation of being too grim and gloomy for races which are essentially wholesome and optimistic in their tendencies. Yet the same period gave the world a series of exquisite pictures from life among the peasant-fishermen on those islands between Stockholm and "the edge of the sea" where Strindberg had previously sought and won the inspiration for his "Master Olof."

Then came the long pause already mentioned. All artistic production was stopped. Scientific speculation took its place, following more and more erratic channels, until it ended in a spell of religious brooding of distinctly morbid type. It was at this time rumor made a Catholic of him. "Lutheranism has been seized by such a panic that Catholics are seen everywhere," Strindberg wrote ten years later in explanation of that rumor. The truth of it was that, guided by Balzac, Swedenborg, Maeterlinck, and the French mystic writer signing himself "Sar" Peladan, he turned from the materialistic creed which had failed to serve his soul as a sheet anchor in the hour of supreme upheaval. When the crisis was over, he stood forth not as a confessor of this or that creed, but as a member of the mystic brotherhood whose mission it is to remind man of the omnipresence of the unknowable. A pessimist he remained even after the dawn of his new faith had set his soul singing once more, but sadness and resignation took the place of bitterness and defiance as the fundamental notes of his soul's melody.

Some of the works included in the appended chronological list stand out beyond the rest either as epoch-making in the author's own career, or as marking a distinct advance on the part of the human spirit in its long struggle to substitute conscious for unconscious growth—and of these alone I shall be able to speak here.

The play "Master Olof" was at first named "The Renegade," and under this title I hope it will become known to the English-speaking world. To Strindberg himself it was largely what "The Pretenders" was to Ibsen—at once a questioning and a formulation of his own genius. The greater modernity of the Swedish work is shown by the fact that its principal hero, who is one of three central figures, fails equally to reach a triumph like that of *King Håkon,* the man divinely commissioned, and to suffer a disaster like that of the self-doubting *Earl*

Skule. Instead he lives on to complete his work—in compromise. To win his way, or rather a way for his mission, he has to sacrifice a part of his vision—and so he is denounced as a renegade by him who sees too far ahead and will sacrifice nothing. This is life, of course; and thus Strindberg may be said to have, for all time, given the true symbolization of the everlasting struggle between the genius and the mass on one side, and between true and false genius on the other.

"The Red Room" is a satirical novel, embodying the conflict between bohemianism and philistinism at Stockholm in the seventies, and written in a vein that shows a rare combination of youthful vigor and merciless satire. But it gives also, as almost all of Strindberg's novels, a detailed study of social conditions in Sweden at that time. Hardly a phase of national existence is unrepresented, and each one of them is sketched in such manner that we also get an idea of the directional tendencies expressed through it. Strindberg's faculty for drawing lifelike pictures not only of individuals but of vast social groups and organisms is among the most striking of his gifts. And to the future historian his novels and autobiographical writings should prove exceedingly valuable.

In the three volumes of short stories named "Swedish Events and Adventures," he made the past of his country a reality no less vital than the one confronting us to-day. The *genre* was by no means new, but none before Strindberg had raised it to quite such perfection. After him similar effects have been achieved with even greater success by Anatole France among others.

The first part of "Marriage" contains a dozen specimens of modern marital unions, presented in a far from unfriendly light. In the preface Strindberg laid out a programme concerning woman's position which vies in radicalism with that for which the women themselves are now fighting all over the world. Not only would he grant

AUGUST STRINDBERG 57

them the suffrage, but he insisted that normal social growth necessitated their having it. But in the second volume of stories issued under the same title, he made a frank attack on two principles generally accepted as essential to woman's complete emancipation, namely the right to hold property, and the right to work at anything for which they can qualify themselves. If their tendency be disregarded, the stories in both volumes will be found to possess high artistic value.

"The Father" was Strindberg's supreme effort to symbolize the life and death struggle between man and woman for such immortality as may be offered them by the child. The picture of that struggle is splendid but unfair. Man, as man, is given rational insight, while to woman is granted little more than low cunning. And as conscience is allied with reason, the victory falls to its unconscionable opponent. It may seem paradoxical to express a regret that the sex problem should enter at all into this play—a play designed wholly to exhaust that very problem. But there is a psychological side to the work that has nothing whatever to do with sex, and this side would hold our interest just as firmly if the conflict were raging between two men. The corrosive power of suggestion is here shown with diabolical skill. It is a duel of souls, with words for weapons, and by a seed of doubt sown in the right way at the right moment, one of those souls is shattered and scattered as fatally as a warship when its magazine explodes.

"Miss Julia," perhaps the most widely known of Strindberg's works, was a frank experiment in new form. Not only are the stage arrangements unconventional, but intermissions have been dispensed with. Naturalism never came nearer to a conquest of the stage, and some of the innovations embodied in this drama are likely to form part of our future dramatic tradition. Again the plot seems to offer us nothing but a sex duel, with the man for winner. But back of *Miss*

AUGUST STRINDBERG 59

Julia and her valet-lover stand two contending strata of humanity—the so-called upper and lower classes. What Strindberg shows us is how a continued process of selective breeding may lead to over-refinement and a weakening of the vital instincts. The racial strain which has reached such a point can find salvation only in mixture with some strain less far removed from the general source of life. If class prejudices or other inhibitive tendencies prevent such a mixture, then the weakened strain will be sloughed off by the race, so that place will be made for other strains with unimpaired vitality and still dormant powers of refinement.

With the novel named "At the Edge of the Sea," Strindberg tried to place himself unreservedly on Nietzschean ground by picturing a superman of to-day and the fate such a man would be likely to suffer at the hands of ordinary humanity. In the course of this attempt, he gave a summary of man's mental development from primal days to the present moment that I count among the most significant and most brilliant pieces of writing contained in modern literature. The principal importance of this novel, however, lies in the fact that Strindberg's merciless logic automatically demolished the glamor of the Nietzschean dream creature. And so this Swedish superman wins in the end nothing but a splendid grave. And his doom is pronounced not by the hostile cunning of the mass, but by his own vain presumption. He fails just as every one must fail who sets out to make others good without their own cooperation. Read in the right way, this novel teaches that supermanhood must be founded on a good deal more of genuine humility than ordinary manhood ever contains.

It was during that middle period of embittered defiance that Strindberg first conceived the idea of a series of autobiographical novels, in which he would adhere closely to his own actual experience while the shock of such self-revelation was to be softened by a change of all proper names. The first volume of this series, issued in 1886 under the title of "The Bondwoman's Son," gives a picture of child life that is full of startling revelations and exquisite interpretations. Strindberg himself has said somewhere that all fiction must be autobiographical in order to obtain full documentary validity. Even if we hold this assertion too sweeping, we must at least grant him to have proved that the most intimate personal experience may be turned into legitimate fiction.

While at all times, to use his own expression, Strindberg "had three strings to his lyre," he appeared during the third period primarily as a dramatist, and it was as such that he preferred to be considered. There is hardly one play from his final period that would not warrant special notice on some account or another. In the eyes of his countrymen, his dramatic presentations of Swedish history have tended to take precedence. And on their account some have dared to call him the Shakespeare of Sweden. But the historical plays of Strindberg are widely different in mettle from that displayed in the "histories" of Shakespeare. No matter how much we find to admire in the latter, they must be held melodramatic in form and rhetorical in expression. They are, in a word, artificial in their portrayal of the past. What Strindberg strove to do—and succeeded in doing, I think—was to reconstruct the everyday aspect of by-gone days. In order to bring the true inwardness as well as lifelike appearance of those days within the ken of our own, he put on the stage not imagined creatures of supernatural size, but plain-speaking men and women of our own kind. But back of these men and women we catch lurid glimpses of big social forces at work. In other words, his works are symbolical in the very best sense of this much misused term—symbolical in the same manner as man's own thinking—and for that reason I believe the day must come when even dramas so intensely national in their subject and spirit as "Gustavus Vasa," "Gustavus Adolphus" and "Charles XII"

AUGUST STRINDBERG 63

will be played and heard in the English-speaking countries.

But for the present his main dramatic contributions to universal literature during this final period must be sought among the plays of modern life, and particularly among those that derived from a frankly acknowledged Maeterlinckian impetus. It was the early Maeterlinck of the puppet plays that set Strindberg once more seeking for a new form. The immediate result of this search was the fairy play "Swanwhite," a very charming but not convincingly original production. Had he stopped there, the charge of imitation sometimes heard might have had some warrant. But to speak of the author of "The Dream Play" or "Toward Damascus" as the imitator of anybody becomes palpably ridiculous the moment you read these works. In both—but especially in the former—he strove to reproduce the kaleidoscopic flexibility and whimsical logic of the dream. And in this way he succeeded as perhaps no one before him to press all life into the narrow confines of a play.

At one time he described "The Dream Play" as a "Buddhistic and proto-Christian drama." Thereby he indicated its underlying philosophy of enlightened resignation and of almost Tolstoyan passivity in the face of violence and injustice and wrong. But we must not be misled by this effort of the matured poet to grasp and vitalize an ideal foreign to his own temperament. "I am a soldier," says *The Hunter* in "The Great Highway," speaking as the *alter ego* of the author; "I am always fighting—fighting to preserve my personal independence." To me the most potent element in "The Dream Play," the one most likely to germinate and survive not only as art but as philosophy, is its tolerant acceptance of every human aspect as an integral part of life. Its main shortcoming lies in a tendency to consider all such aspects as established for all future. Viewing life statically, however, and not kinetically—from the realist's viewpoint rather than from the idealist's—it will prove difficult to find an artistic symbolization of it more subtle or more convincing than that given us in "The Dream Play."

Although the trilogy "Toward Damascus" is autobiographical in source as well as purpose—a sort of gigantic private reckoning worked out by one deeming himself too seriously tried by life—its appeal is nevertheless universal. We may forget the fate of him who projected those mighty dramatic cloud-shapes, and read out of them nothing but a masterly record of the stumbling progress made by a human soul in its search for harmonious correlation of its own conflicting elements—its desires and aspirations, its selfish and unselfish tendencies. In the third part we find *Father Melchior* calling out to the Strindbergian protagonist, here named *The Stranger*: "You began life by affirming everything; you continued it by denying everything. End it now with a coordination. Therefore, cease to be exclusive! Say not 'either—or,' but say instead 'both—and!'" Here we have Strindberg's onward march through forty years of thinking and working outlined in a couple of sentences—and we cannot fail to recognize its identity with the general course of human progress, which runs from blind belief through arrogant denial to a reasoned balancing of faith and doubt.

Close as the trilogy must have stood to what was Strindberg's innermost self, there is a professedly objective work that seems to have come still closer, though in a different manner—a work where Strindberg's artistic aloofness makes us almost forget that, in spite of it, he was still dealing with his own spiritual experiences, and with nothing else. This work, the double play named "The Dance of Death," I am often inclined to count the crowning climax of his production, the work in which his always remarkable art reached its highest potency of perfection. It is as closely knit as a

Greek drama or a play by Ibsen at his best. Only three characters figure in the first part, and five in the second. There are only two settings—one for each part. The dialogue has rarely, if ever, been surpassed for combined incisiveness and verisimilitude. Incident leads to incident with a fatality that vainly tries to mask its logic behind the leering face of chance. Some of the scenes are among the most tensely dramatic that may be found in modern literature, and yet the total impression is just what the author seems to have aimed at: a sense of the hopeless monotony underlying life's superficial disturbances.

A piece of most delicate, and yet most deep-reaching symbolism (outwardly expressed by the round form of the room in which the action takes place) lies in the circular movement of the first part, whereby everything becomes reduced once more to the state of the opening scene. All the tumult of living is brought back to a pitiful striving at self-assertion on the part of the individual. Yet the suggestion is always present, that in all his seemingly futile striving the individual takes the place of a puppet in the hands of some higher power, working for great aims that he cannot perceive. Life and hell are rendered almost synonymous, but the Swedenborgian idea of hell as a state of mind is not for a moment left out of sight. The one possible agent of escape is the Hogarthian fiddler, always hovering on the horizon like a storm cloud before which all cower in panic. But when he comes at last and brings the dance to a close, he is seen to bring with him pardon and peace, mercy and harmony. One of the figures in the play, *Curt,* might be called the superman of Strindberg's final period: a touching incarnation of the struggle between reasoned humility and instinctive pride that was always raging in the author's own breast. But the most striking figure of all is that of *The Captain,* the embodiment of ruthless self-concern, to whom nevertheless is given the pronouncement of

Strindberg's ultimate philosophical creed: "Wipe out and pass on!"

Few works produced by Strindberg brought him harsher criticism in his native country than the two novels "The Gothic Rooms" and "Black Flags," which served him as vent pipes for a gathering wrath. During the last decade of his life the relationship between himself and certain contemporary writers approaching close to him in rank was always more or less strained, until, a few years before his death, it led to an outburst of bitter polemics known in Swedish literary history as the "Strindberg feud." To some extent the fault was his own. Largely, however, it lay with his rivals, who all too often let personal prejudice and jealousy dictate judgments that should have been concerned with nothing but actual merit. Whether it be ever wise for the injured in such cases to protest in person is a question not easy to decide. And in making his protests, Strindberg frequently shot over the mark, or even went so far as to make capital out of the private lives of his supposed or real enemies. But with every allowance made for the doubtful aspects of the two works mentioned above, there remains in them a residuum of merit and of broad appeal that will probably insure them approval from a time that shall have forgotten the personal accusations now read between their lines. Even at his worst, Strindberg was one of the great. And though he might be cruelly unjust to rivals or enemies, he rarely failed in his exact observation of the generation to which he belonged. If that generation was sick of soul or loose of living, the blame can hardly be laid on the man who merely discovered and proclaimed the sickness and the sin.

Of "Inferno," his most original effort at autobiographical fiction, I have already spoken. In 1903 he wrote another volume in the same series, "Alone," which might be called the antithesis of his previous record of wandering through a self-made hell. It is a piece of pure poetry—the autumnal reverie of a man who, at last, has made his peace with the world and paid the price for it. And in this volume Strindberg's marvellous power of word-painting stands revealed in all its glory.

I cannot end this all too brief characterization of Strindberg's main works without calling attention to an additional and somewhat confusing aspect of his passion for self-revelation. Not satisfied with giving us a detailed story of his life and artistic development, he wrote also stories of the story, revelations of how previous revelations had come to be made. In a number of pamphlets, and particularly in those quaint collections of notes, sketches, aphorisms and speculations which he named "Blue Books," material of this kind was piled up at a tremendous rate, until the image to be evoked became blurred by the superabundance of fact used to evoke it. I wonder, however, whether this condition may not alter as passing time places everything in proper perspective. For it would seem that concern-

ing a mind so rich and so original, both in
its coloring and in its tendencies, the amount
of available data could hardly become too
great.

The influence exercised by Strindberg on
the literature of his native country was tremendous—the very language of Sweden
seemed to take on new color and vigor
through his audacious use of its more colloquial elements. Until he appeared Sweden
could hardly be said to have a literature of
international appeal. With his appearance
began a new era of startling fertility and
variety. For the first time the country
possessed a native drama of genuine merit,
and to the novel an impetus was given which
is still making itself felt and of which the
richest fruits may yet remain ungarnered.
For a long time Strindberg was the sole
model: all the others were mere *epigoni*.
And even when a new movement, which
might be called neo-romantic because of its
mystical and lyrical undercurrents, devel-

oped from a hostile reaction against the exaggerated naturalism of some among his followers, Strindberg himself was among the first to prove himself a master of the new mood. Thus he remained a leader to the very end, though no longer the only one as he was in the beginning.

But no matter how great a writer may appear to his immediate surroundings, or how valuable his services may be to the literature of his own country, something more is wanted to insure him a place in that larger field where community of blood and tongue is no longer a consideration. Almost from the start of his career as writer, however, Strindberg displayed qualities capable of carrying his name and fame beyond the borders of his native land. Norway and Denmark were, naturally enough, the first foreign countries to acclaim his rising star, but almost at the same time its rays were discovered in Germany. And in Germany Strindberg remains to this day recognized as one of the principal builders of the literature which is most characteristic of our own day. And there is good reason to believe that the naturalistic movement, which seems to have been an inevitable phase of the last century's literary development everywhere, reached Germany through Strindberg and the Dane Jacobsen rather than through direct imitation of French models, the ground having been prepared for it by an eager study of Dickens.

Of what Strindberg may have given, or failed to give, to the spirit of his age, I shall speak later. At present I am only concerned with his contributions to form. Regarding his life-work in its entirety, his main contributions of this kind seem to have been: first, a breaking down of old conventions whereby both the novel and the drama, in their design as well as in their expression, were rendered more truly life-like; and, secondly, an intensification of the psychological analysis by application of scientific discoveries so recent that they are only just now becoming the property of the average thinking layman.

It has been said that his characters do nothing but quarrel, that they are too busy abusing each other to really live. I might suggest a comparative study of a writer like Galsworthy, and I think such a study would reveal that even the gentle irony and wonderful balance of the man who gave us "The Country House" and "Fraternity" fail to keep the dignified, self-complacent characters of "upper" England from spending much of their time and energy on the futile game of incrimination and recrimination. Here as elsewhere, I fear the fault is with life and not with Strindberg. *His* fault it was simply to picture us as we are rather than as we should like to be thought—and we are still a lot of self-centred, grasping, bad-tempered children. Of course, he did dwell on the unlovely sides of our characters and manners with rather morbid preoccupation, but he did so because he thought us sick, dead, damned souls, whose one way to health and life and salvation lay through a road now being preached in this country as the one reliable panacea—namely *publicity*.

Whether his figures quarrel or caress each other—as they sometimes will do, and then most convincingly—there is in their quick, brisk utterances a sound as of hammer-blows on an anvil. And about their actions and feelings, their thoughts and words, there is a circumspect directness, if I so may name it, that is otherwise to be found only in real life. Their talk may wander, their actions may be ever so disingenuous or hypocritical—about their motives there can rarely be any question, and what they say or do is sure to be what will best serve those motives.

Now and then Strindberg would preach brazenly, and use his figures most mercilessly for his private purposes, but even then they remain natural. Take, for instance, one of the long harangues delivered either by *Gustav* or *Adolph* in "Creditors." Is there one man among us so short of breath or firm of temper that he has never broken out into some such stream of fermenting and corrosive, or merely apologetic, phrases? And even when, in the course of one such outburst, *Adolph* begins by saying that he has only been *Tekla's* lover, but not her husband, and ends by exclaiming that, as he cannot be her lover, he is going to be her husband whether she likes it or not, this implies no mistake on the part of *Adolph's* creator, but a particularly shrewd reproduction of the way our minds wander when lashed by certain emotional storm winds.

I can think of few writers who have equalled Strindberg's acuteness in distinguishing the subtlest nuances within the ever-shifting human soul. One of the reasons why he seems almost childish at times to some readers is just that he sees so clearly what usually lies hidden within the innermost recesses of the soul, and that he describes what he sees with such gruesome accuracy. Mental processes that in the average man seem incapable of rising above the threshold of the subconscious, seemed within him to push boldly into the full light of self-consciousness, and what he tells us of them has the strange aspect of forms until then deemed wholly chimerical. The very idea that such things may exist within us is resented.

What I have just said applies equally to the realms of head and heart, to our emotions and our thoughts. All human possibilities—even the most inhuman—lie dormant within every one of us; and now and then some of the worst among them will rear their poisonous fangs in a moment of lowered vitality or relaxed vigilance. Where Strindberg failed, perhaps, was not in his insistence on their presence, but in his doubt of our ability to push them back into the primeval darkness whence they have followed us like shadows—inalienable, and yet no longer true parts of our more human selves.

To prove these contentions of mine would take more space than I can dispose of for

AUGUST STRINDBERG 79

the present. A random example must suffice—even though it be not as typical as I might wish. The behavior of *Miss Julia* has often been attacked as too unwomanly, or too pathological for legitimate poetical use. The nature of that behavior the reader must discover for himself in the play. All I want to point out here is that Strindberg undertook to picture a type which, while existing everywhere and having particular validity during the present transitory stage of the social organism, yet stands distinctly apart from the main mass of humanity. This type, developed by the over-breeding of some racial strain, constitutes a serious problem to-day.

"Miss Julia" was written and published in 1888. The first edition of Sir Francis Galton's "Inquiries into Human Faculty" saw the light five years earlier, to be sure, but I don't think it made much of a public stir at first, and I am sure that it was quite unknown to Strindberg in 1888. In this work its author speaks of "the diminished fertility of highly-bred animals," and adds that in them "together with infertility is combined some degree of sexual indifference, or when passion is shown, it is not unfrequently for some specimen of a coarser type." In this single sentence, coming from one of the most painstaking students of our own age, is contained all the justification that can ever be required for the existence of *Miss Julia*.

Yet I do not for a moment mean to insist that Strindberg was always perfect, or even reasonably correct. He was too impetuous, too impassioned, too high-strung, not to stray from the truth at times. A far from hostile Swedish critic, Tor Hedberg, reproached him once for his "blind faith in the value of even the most fleeting impulse." And he, of whose painstaking efforts at exactness I have already spoken, was sometimes outright slovenly in his carelessness. His over-confidence in his own memory accounts for some of this shortcoming; his preoccupation with large outlines and sweep-

AUGUST STRINDBERG

ing truths, for more; his method of working and the circumstances under which he worked, for still more.

From the first he was beset with economical worries. At once generous and impractical, he was unable to make money stay in his hands. Really enormous sums passed through those hands, and yet he was always in difficulty. And the demands on him were ever growing. As early as the first half of the eighties—the period of "Marriage" and "Real Utopias," of "The Secret of the Guild" and "The New Kingdom"—he was so hard pressed that he had to send out his manuscripts without even looking them over. His very consciousness of neglect bred an almost irresistible aversion to the reading of his own work until long after its production.

Nor did he ponder or hesitate while producing it. Like one of the old vikings, he attacked rather than essayed his task. Returning from a brisk morning walk, he would strip to the waist and then write without pause for about four hours. Hardly ever would he turn back to erase or correct. Everything seemed to flow from some inner storehouse where it had been lying ready for external materialization. Considering this, what should be wondered at is not his occasional slips, but the marvellous accuracy and agility of a mind that could in such fashion produce works like "The Dance of Death," where the dialogue is intricate in its texture as the famous web of Penelope, and yet inexorable as fate itself in its progress toward the predestined goal.

So far the effect of Strindberg's influence outside of Sweden has shown itself most markedly on the stage. The drama as we have it to-day, in plays like those of Shaw, Galsworthy, Granville Barker and the late St. John Hankin, must be held the joint production of Ibsen and Strindberg. Others—men like Björnson and Maeterlinck—have been among the master builders, but in almost every instance the determining im-

'pulse to liberation and innovation came from one of the two spirits who, in spite of innumerable differences, had so much in common. One wrought with the quick, fiery leap of a hungry flame; the other, with the grinding deliberation of a glacier. The result was the same in each case: new life, truer life, more intense life. Ibsen gave more to the spirit of the drama, Strindberg more to its form. It was the rather tragic destiny of the latter to create instruments of exquisite precision which he himself could not always use to best advantage.

As early as 1872, when he was only twenty-three, he did in his "Master Olof" what, nearly twenty years later, Shaw did more pleasantly but no more convincingly in "Cæsar and Cleopatra." When, in 1888, he wrote his famous preface to "Miss Julia," advocating naturalistic reforms for the stage, he was hopelessly in advance of his time. To-day those ideas have become so largely accepted in the best playhouses that to many people they seem like outlived commonplaces when read for the first time in English. When those ideas were just beginning their triumphant conquest of the stage, Strindberg was already advocating new forms of still more daring realism—the suggestive, symbolical realism that has become most closely associated with the names of Gordon Craig and Georg Fuchs.

We may be opposed to the spirit of much that he has written. Other artists will study and repeat his form, pouring into it the spirit which their own day demands—the spirit out of which the unborn soul of the future is to be shaped. Thus, and thus only, the torch is handed on from generation to generation. For to no man, however great, is it granted to give everything; and from no man have we the right to exact absolute perfection as the sole condition of our approval.

III

His Spirit

THE process of gradual displacement and substitution which we call progress seems invariably to result from a conflict between opposed but complementary principles. Of such antagonisms life holds any number. But out of the mass a few emerge as more vital and deep-going than the rest. In the spiritual life of man, as we find it embodied in his speculative and imaginative literatures, there are three predominant antagonisms of this kind. As the human mind swings toward one side or the other across these lines of everlasting cleavage, we obtain certain universal moods, or ways of looking at life, that we name respectively: 1) realism and idealism; 2) individualism and socialism; 3) scepticism and mysticism.

Realism insists that, in the last instance, art must always fall back on concrete existence for its material. Idealism maintains that, after all, the highest purpose of art is to use the material thus obtained for the creation of new life. In other words, realism looks mainly to the present moment, and idealism to the future; realism to what is, idealism to what should be.

Individualism emphasizes the cellular construction of all society, and the dependence of social welfare on the free development of each cell—that is, of the individual. Socialism prefers to accentuate the visible and invisible connections that bind all the cells together into a larger unit, and that render their individual welfare dependent on the harmonious development of the social organism in its entirety.

Scepticism sees life as a concrete multiplicity. It clings to the relativity of all being and has for its aim to save man from spiritual stagnation by revealing to him the insufficiency of every truth already established. To mysticism, on the other hand, life appears and appeals primarily as an abstract unity, and it serves to save man from spiritual chaos by urging him to shape the fragments of shattered truths into new ones of nobler aspect and wider application.

The character of this threefold array of distinctions makes it plain that we are not dealing with certain falsehoods to be overcome and certain truths to be established in their place. Realism and idealism, for instance, are equally *true,* which simply means that they are equally needful to the orderly workings of human reason, and also to the effective comprehension of the problem of living. They may be said to represent two juxtaposed viewpoints from which life may be observed. And in order to grasp life in its fullness, in all its protean complexity, man must endeavor to do the impossible—he must try to behold life and all it contains from both those antipodal points at the same time. Progress, or the mind's continued swinging back and forth between these points, cannot, therefore, have for its purpose any complete elimination of the principles involved, but must rather be looked upon as aiming at the gradual merging of the essential elements in each pair of opposites into a synthetic whole. And it is only reasonable to conclude that the greatness of men and periods alike may be measured by the extent to which they succeed in such a synthetic embodiment of theretofore prevailing antagonisms.

What we call genius implies most frequently, of course, a supremely satisfactory embodiment of the momentary swing of the racial mind toward one extreme or the other. Less frequently, but even more characteristically, it implies a foreshadowing of the impending reversal of the racial mind's momentary bias. But rarest and greatest that form of genius must be held which mirrors in its expressions both what is and what will come, so that it implies not a one-sided development, but an organic fusion of some dualism that cuts all the rest of life in twain.

AUGUST STRINDBERG

Among the salient qualities in Strindberg's character—inherited or developed by reaction against his environment—none seems to have been more determining for the spirit informing his work than that which he himself named his "sensitiveness to pressure." Implying, as it did, an over-concern about his own self, a fear that the world might violate and overwhelm what he held most typical of his selfhood, and becoming, as it also did, morbidly exaggerated in times of physical and psychical depression, it kept him throughout life in a state of internal and external conflict.

It prevented him from ever feeling at peace either with the surrounding world or with his own purposes. It was the main cause of the tragedy which ran so unmistakably through his whole life. It colored his relationship to every one with whom he came in contact, and especially to the women with whose assistance he sought to overcome his own fate. It kept him a stranger and an outcast within a generation whose innermost soul-secrets he laid bare in his work. It kept him, too, vainly seeking for happiness while the fretful voice within was whispering all the time that happiness is unattainable and should not be sought for. And strange as it may seem, when said of one so dogmatic in his utterances, it made it impossible for him, even when he strove most pathetically, to surrender himself unconditionally to any one current or attitude, the frequent result of any such effort being that he raised his voice still more clamorously to drown the nagging doubt within.

This quality produced beyond doubt a greater degree of restlessness than was good for the normal development of his art. It served largely to create that atmosphere of disharmony and fruitless excitement which mars some of his best work. But it was also responsible for that wonderful alertness and agility of mind which the world was inclined to condemn as mere instability. It kept his spirit always "on the move," always searching for an abiding place of rest that was never found, always ready to see "the other side" of any standpoint momentarily assumed. But just such a mind, so prone to find any accepted conviction empty and irksome, would be particularly fitted to become the typical incarnation of a century like the nineteenth, with its nervous striving after concreteness, its fear of being held the dupe of life, and its haunting dread that evolution and progress might in the end prove alien to each other.

It is not to be wondered, then, that Strindberg's art as a rule, though not always, embodied less of the fusion toward which life's integral antagonisms are eternally tending, than of the conflict, the violent swinging back and forth from one onesidedness to another, by which such a fusion is gradually to be attained. But as he threw himself with equal ardor now to this side and now to that, into sceptical realism or mystical idealism, he managed with marvellous accuracy to reflect or foreshadow a corresponding movement by the race-mind of the western world. Sometimes he followed; more often he led: but however startling his attitude might seem to the superficial glance of the unthinking, he was never out of touch with the prevailing spiritual trend of his day—except possibly at a single point: in his attitude toward women and their new aspirations toward a life more expressive of their own natures. The very abruptness of his transition from one viewpoint to another, as well as the arrogance with which he maintained the final validity of each new one, was characteristic of a time which, by its scientific and philosophical conquests, had been rendered incapable of remaining satisfied for long with any position representing only a single aspect of the many-sided truth at the centre of things.

Of the antipodal points defined above, there was not one toward which Strindberg did not tend at one period or another. By turns he sought the truth that lies on the surface and that which is hidden rather than revealed by outward appearances; by turns he spurned the mass and the individual; by turns he sought the secret spring of existence in the adventitious movement of atoms and in the omniscient plans of a divine principle. But through all his seeming self-contradictions ran nevertheless a certain inward consistency, showing that while he might seek different goals at different times, the motives that kept him on the search were pretty nearly identical throughout. Thus, for instance, while his pendular movement from socialism to individualism and back again was accompanied by an inner stress gaining almost tragic strength and resulting in a proportionate outward emphasis, he was emotionally always an individualist. His reason alone, taking its start from an uncommonly acute observation of surrounding conditions, enabled him to realize the possibility of individuals existing for the sake of the race, or of life in its entirety, rather than for the sake of any purposes harbored within themselves. But action on this realization was invariably resisted by a spirit of self-sufficiency and self-concern that brooked no ultimate denial.

His scepticism was as deeply rooted as his individualism—but so was also his mysticism, although for a long while he did his best to suppress it. He had always to doubt something and to believe in something else—and he doubted and believed with equal fervor. During his period of complete religious denial, his allegiance to science and its formulas had in it a touch of superstition. When, at the hands of Swedenborg, he re-entered those mysterious regions where life's concrete multiplicity seems to vanish before the glory of its abstract unity, he turned his inevitable scepticism against science—while at the same time he was using scientific methods and data in proving that powers of which we wot nothing are carrying us to deserved destinies along roads that we can neither foretell nor avoid.

From this we can only conclude that, in spite of all exaggeration, there was in him, by virtue of his very restlessness, a tendency to master that synthetic position toward which, in my belief, the race-mind is to-day particularly striving. The increasing rapidity of our oscillations during the past century seems to suggest our approach to a point where the main business in hand will be the reduction of life's everlasting disharmonies into a state of temporary and comparative harmony. It must be a harmony at once shortlived and deceptive. Yet it will be of tremendous importance as the starting point of new conflicts, operating on a higher level than that which is now dropping behind us. It would be a gross injustice to Strindberg to overlook the presence in his work of definite signs foreshadowing the impending truce. Arch-individualist as he was to the last, he counted among his fundamental axioms that no human soul can exist without constructive interaction with other human souls. And when, late in life, he wanted to sum up the lesson of all history as read by himself, he did so in the words: "Everything serves!"

In fact, he managed at almost every juncture to take a position of compromise in regard to at least one of the three main antagonisms. And his efforts at coordination were most marked in his final and greatest period, although at the beginning of his career as artist his attitude toward life and its problems showed much more balance than during the long desert wandering of the middle period. As we behold his work in such plays, for example, as "The Dance of Death" or "The Dream Play," it has passed far beyond the largely photographic verisimilitude and the weakness for enumeration of detail which characterized so much of what we generally call naturalistic literature. He was always a realist, clinging closely to actual existence both in form and choice of subject-matter. But the longer he lived and worked, the more his realism became spiritual rather than material in its type. And in his latest stage it rose time and again to that kind of suggestive impressionism which I prefer to name symbolism, and which enables the mind to reconstruct the desired picture out of a few salient contours.

It must be admitted that the impression of Strindberg's thought as well as of his form frequently has a puzzling effect even on those long familiar with both. There are passages and situations in his works of every period that seem so quaintly naïve as to make their author suspected of sheer childishness. And again there are times when the impartial reader can think of only one word as fit for the man so often reckoned the most modern of moderns. This word is "old-fashioned." But I, for one, have discovered that the supposed naïveté may be a result of rare courage, enabling its possessor to brush aside all our common artificialities and sophistications, thereby imparting to his art an atmosphere of simple and serene majesty. And, partly against my own inclination, I have been forced to conclude that what now strikes us as out of date may turn out to be far in advance of the time.

There was, as I have already intimated, one point at which, during the greater part of his life, Strindberg seemed surprisingly out of touch with contemporary thought. In a period that witnessed the sudden maturing of modern feminism into a world-encircling movement of irresistible power, he assumed an attitude toward woman and her new aspirations that earned him the title of misogynist and caused much of the opposition he undeniably had to encounter during the most critical part of his life. It was not his original attitude. Being a man moved in the last instance by emotional reactions and personal considerations, he began by worshipping woman as a higher and purer being than man. Thereby he betrayed his romantic origins. What caused his change of front I have already described. The radical character of that change made many people forget that from love to hatred is only a step, while both are far removed from indifference. And no matter how bitterly Strindberg might abuse and curse woman, she remained always one of his chief preoccupations.

Of course, he denied on several occasions that he had ever felt any hatred against the other sex: all he wanted was to reduce woman to her proper position! Such a desire, however, lies really at the bottom of everything called hatred, which is nothing but apprehension on behalf of one's own sense of superiority. And Strindberg spoke more than once of women in words warranting still harsher terms of condemnation. "Woman is always in the wrong when opposing man, because he is the man, and she is an appendage to him," he said, for example, in "The Gothic Rooms," published as late as 1904. What he charged her with was not only a moral, but an actual biological inferiority. Thus the novel "At the Edge of the Sea," dating back to 1890, contains a reference to "that intermediary form between man and child which is called woman;" while seventeen years later, in "Black Flags," he again asserted that "woman follows man in the evolutionary chain and precedes the child."

This remarkable opinion, which also found a more practical expression in his violent opposition to "the modern woman's mania for earning her own living," was, of course, largely referable to that "sensitiveness to pressure" of which I have already had to speak more than once. This is proved by his own admission in "Toward Damascus," where *The Stranger* remarks that he had perhaps "been jealous of his own personality, fearful lest he fall under some outside influence." It is still more strikingly proved and illuminated by a passage in "The Gothic Rooms," where *Esther* asks her mystic lover, *Count Max*, to name his greatest joy in life, and he answers: "Giving birth to a new thought, for then I am both father and mother, and I need not share the honor with some woman who may run away with my child, saying it is hers."

In this matter my own position is diametrically opposed to that of Strindberg. I have not the slightest desire to endorse his views on womanhood, and feel hardly able to defend them, but I do wish to understand and interpret them, no matter how widely they happen to differ from my own. And in a man of his calibre I am inclined to regard the most eccentric opinions as symptomatic of some overlooked social necessity or racial tendency, rather than of blindness or malice. Nor is it to be overlooked in this connection, that views strongly reminiscent of Strindberg's, though less extravagantly expressed, have been found in the works of men like H. G. Wells and Robert Herrick, none of whom can by any stretch of imagination be classed as a misogynist.

Primarily Strindberg's attitude was a personal reaction, as I have already suggested, but life stands always ready to make use of our private little likes and dislikes for the furthering of its own inscrutable purposes. And I believe that we are here in the presence of a new racial movement, tending less to oppose the emancipation of woman than to arouse man to a fuller understanding of his own nature and mission. For ages the world was man-ruled—so much so that any undermining of the male supremacy seemed inconceivable. This condition had, in the end, the effect of helping the feministic agitation that has now been carried on with growing intensity and success for more than a century. For while the men were opposed to the demands made by the women, their opposition took merely the form of passive indifference, as they never dreamt that their own power might become endangered.

That to-day we may talk of a decided "feminization" of the world, I regard as unquestionable. Personally I do not regret this process, which I hold both inevitable and beneficial, but I can nevertheless easily imagine the future development of it to a point where the correcting influence of the male spirit might become practically annulled. I am not having in mind anything so ridiculous as the possible subjugation of man by woman, but the establishment of onesided ideals tending to rob the race of the impetus toward variation, innovation and abstraction commonly supposed to inhere in the male character.

The man who, as Strindberg did in "At the Edge of the Sea," could refer to the ideal woman imaged by one of his heroes as "a woman born with intelligence enough to recognize the inferiority of her own sex to the other one," seems to me at once something more and something less than a misogynist or anti-feminist. If a label he must have, it would be better to make it *masculinist*. Strindberg was, in fact, a frank upholder of the intrinsic superiority of his own sex, and as such vehemently and instinctively opposed to the equally frank feminism of men like Ibsen and Björnson.

Thanks to his almost preternatural sensitiveness to any impending alteration of racial tendencies, he may have foreseen the possibility I have just outlined. And thanks to his private relationship to various women bent on resisting his encroachments upon their own individualities, if not on attempting an invasion of his, he may also have been moved more quickly and more powerfully than others to oppose the danger which, at the worst, must be lying in the lap of a still unborn day. Read in this light, I think much in his work that now seems unintelligible or objectionable may appear worthy of more serious consideration. And the lesson to be drawn from that element in his work would prompt no futile efforts at suppression of the woman movement, but should instead lead to a more conscious preservation and cultivation of certain qualities held to be particularly characteristic of masculinity, if not of manhood. Out of the more evenly balanced conflict between aroused masculinism and liberated feminism the race would then by degrees issue at another kind of synthesis or compromise which might appropriately be named *humanism.*

Before leaving this phase of Strindberg's art, I wish to point out that his attitude toward woman, as toward everything else in life, had its modifications and qualifications, some of which were determined by reason and others by sentiment. Speaking of his fairy play "Swanwhite," a Swedish critic has remarked that "one is surprised to find him painting a female figure with nothing but light, attractive and joyous colors." The explanation is quite simple. In spite of the charming love story that runs through the play in question, the little *Princess Swanwhite* is primarily pictured as daughter, and not as mistress or mate. To her creator she was a child to the end— one of those blessed beings whom he worshipped when all the rest of mankind seemed hateful.

About the woman with matured powers he

night write as he did in "Toward Damascus" (Part III): "I sought in woman an angel who was to lend me wings, and I fell into the arms of the earth spirit, who smothered me among pillows she had filled with her own wing feathers." (Compare this with what Robert Herrick makes one of his female characters say in "The Healer": "We women are but chance vessels for a man's will—or devils to destroy him when he proves to be less than man.") Even woman as a mother was not free from his fierce questioning and fiercer accusations, as he showed in the one-act play "Mother-Love," and again in such a late production as the "chamber play" named "The Pelican." In the latter case, however, we must bear in mind that what he really assailed was hypocrisy, and that his main thesis was that no human feeling is sacred enough to protect it against abuse. But, to return to the point I wanted to make, against the child, whatever its sex, he could never employ that blasting power of invective which otherwise spared nothing.

And two of his happiest efforts, the fairy plays "Lucky-Pehr's Journey" and "The Slippers of Abu Casem," were prompted by his desire to please two favorite daughters of his own, one of whom I believe also to have inspired the figure of *Swanwhite* which so surprised the Swedish critic.

There are two distinct currents—not opposed, but parallel—discernible in Strindberg's later work. One of these moves on the surface. It is concerned with the means rather than the end, with the road rather than the goal. It brings us back to those strange soul-adventures by which he found his way to a "full, rock-firm certitude," declared by himself, not long before his death, to have been the chief gain of his middle-age crisis. The elements entering into this current are not only mystical but occult. They are derived in part from Swedenborg, and in part from the picturesque French dreamer and mystic signing himself "Sar" Peladan. But principally they must have sprung from Strindberg's own experience in moments of abnormal tension.

What happened to him, or seemed to happen at least, when he was striving to make gold by the transmutation of baser metals, and what he described to us with such bewildering exactitude in his "Inferno" and "Legends," has become objectively projected in the rest of his work from that period. The world without is deeply colored by the purple flame within. Coincidence is law. It is the fingerpoint of Providence, the signal to man that he must beware. Mystery is the gospel: the mystery implied in the knitting together of man to man, of fact to fact, deep beneath the surface of things. Few writers could take us into such a realm of probable impossibilities and possible improbabilities without losing all claim to serious consideration. If Strindberg thus ventured to our gain and no loss of his own, his success can be explained only by the presence in his work of that second, deeper current of thought and feeling.

AUGUST STRINDBERG 109

This is as simple as the current nearer the surface is fantastic. It is the tangible embodiment of that "rock-firm certitude" to which I have already referred. It is the faith which he strove to make his own during youth, and which, as earnestly, he strove to deny and demolish during early manhood. Of its character and his new look upon it he spoke as follows in one of his late pamphlets ("Religious Renascence") : "In the 'Blue Books' I have returned to Christianity as the only form of spiritual life possible *to me*. In my great need I took what was ready at hand; and instructed by Swedenborg that a man is born into the religion of his country as well as into its nationality, I adopted as postulate (or sheet anchor) the faith into which I had been baptized and confirmed. With a little good will, I got reason into the dogmas and accepted everything. From this I suffered no harm; but I could as well have taken my Christianity without dogmas—with only the Bible as basis, and without any reasoning about it.

And that is what I am doing at this moment."

Elsewhere (in his "Speeches to the Swedish Nation") he has given this explanation of what religion meant to himself, and what he felt it ought to mean to others: "Only through religion, or the hope of something better, and the recognition of the innermost meaning of life as that of an ordeal, a school, or perhaps a penitentiary, will it be possible to bear the burden of life with sufficient resignation."

It is thoroughly in keeping with Strindberg's nature and its queer blend of complexity and simplicity, that, at the beginning of the twentieth century, he should insist on believing in a personal deity and its direct interference in human affairs, while at the same time the object of his religious faith was purely moral. For a moralist he was first of all, and he was so inevitably by virtue of that emotional undercurrent which, to my mind, gave the primary impetus to all his actions and reactions. It was the same

whether he dealt with religion or politics—
for even when he called himself a socialist,
he was thinking much more of duties than
of rights. And this passion of his for the
plain and humble virtues of life, for frank-
ness and kindness and square dealing between man and man, never left him, never
abated its ardor. It stayed with him
throughout that middle period which he himself looked upon with regret and disap-
proval. Even then he was not much of an
atheist, as several remarks by *Gustav* in
"Creditors" prove amply; even then he held
the faith which he thought lost, as is shown
in the same play when *Tekla* suggests that
a belief in a Providence or in a blind fate
has the same effect of relieving man from all
liability, and *Gustav* answers:

"To some extent, yes, but there is always
a narrow margin left unprotected, and there
the liability applies in spite of all. And
sooner or later the creditors make their appearance. Guiltless, but responsible. Guiltless in regard to him who is no more;

responsible to oneself and one's fellow-beings!"

Both in the world of art and in that of thought, Strindberg undoubtedly had original ideas to offer. He was, for instance, one of the first among modern thinkers who dared, in the face of abuse and ridicule, to maintain the underlying unity of the elements and their probable transmutability, and he did so on strictly scientific grounds, thereby forestalling the position since then arrived at by Sir William Ramsay and others. His misfortune was that neither one of those worlds was really his own. Beauty was needful to him, but not all-sufficient. Truth fascinated him always, even when it appeared as its own only object, but it could never in that form outlive his impetuous craving for application. Sooner or later he would always return to the ethical view of life, to the question of right and wrong—and in this field, though most dear to him, he had nothing original to offer, nothing that compared with Ibsen's prophetic reinterpretation of human duties and desires.

But Strindberg's contribution to the art of living—which is, after all, the proper name for applied ethics—must not on this account be scorned or slighted. It was his mission to turn us back to truths and virtues so overlaid with the dust of philosophical discussion that they had grown nearly invisible. Being a sentimentalist he was an incurable rebel. But as he lived in a time when to be orthodox was to question all that the past had believed in, his rebellion drove him back into that very past in search of the firm ground his spirit craved. There is nothing to be regretted in this. The movement of all life is cyclic. We never return to the point once passed, but after a time we are certain to draw near to it in order to pick, from above, what the law of compensation forced us to surrender temporarily as price for our passing of that point. Thus the ascending spiral of progress is formed.

What we may regret about Strindberg's

spirit is that, in his return to the past for lost treasures, he could not carry with him more of the light gained by the race along the road he retraced. I am thinking of his essential pessimism, which he never outlived. He was brave, no doubt, but his bravery in face of life and its problems did not rise above resignation. And such an attitude of submission to a fate over which we have no power whatever does not satisfy to-day's humanity. Even at that, however, he had much to teach us, and in particular three things: 1) that man is part of a larger whole, and not an end in himself; 2) that duties are of much greater importance than rights, both to ourselves and to the rest of life; 3) that this life grows meaningless unless we accept it as a preparation for something lying beyond and above it. And as Strindberg was never dogmatic about either the causes or purposes of life, as long as such causes and purposes were admitted to exist, it should be possible for us to receive what he brought us out of the past and to use it in our own way—the way of a time that seems about to realize how far the essence of all wisdom lies in seeking the truth along more than one road.

In trying to fathom and estimate the spirit of Strindberg, let us always bear in mind the indubitable sincerity and tremendous earnestness which stamped all he did and said as with a seal of fire. He was one of those rare few who always meant what he said, and who meant it with all there was in him of emotional and intellectual power. Too implicitly, perhaps, he believed in the validity of his own mission, and unnecessarily, perhaps, he believed that silence always stood for approval when big matters were at stake. But his sense of mission was combined with a never-resting self-distrust that, at the best, made him regard himself as a tool chastised for purposes of better service. And his themes gripped deeply and strongly into life as actually lived. He was always dealing with things that *matter,* and mostly with things that matter vastly. Every mood was known to him, the tenderest as well as the harshest. Generally a certain stern grimness prevailed with him, but no matter how sternly he might deal with others, there was none of whom he demanded so much as of himself. In more respects than one he was comparable to one of those loud-voiced and sharp-tongued old Hebrew prophets, whose temper and language he seemed to share in equal degree. Once he was named by a critic the artistic conscience of his own country. But as I see him, he shared with Ibsen and Tolstoy the soul-saddening task of being the spiritual conscience of the entire period to which he belonged—a period which we have outlived, but whose lessons we have still to master.

IV

A REVISED LIST OF AUGUST STRINDBERG'S WORKS ARRANGED IN CHRONOLOGICAL ORDER

Plays

1869-85. The Freethinker. Hermione. In Rome. The Outlaw. A. D. Forty-eight. Master Olof (or The Renegade); two versions. The Secret of the Guild. Sir Bengt's Lady. Lucky-Pehr's Journey.

1886-96. The People at Hemsö. The Father. Miss Julia. Comrades. Creditors. Pariah. Simoom. The Stronger. Playing with Fire. The Link. Facing Death. The First Warning. Debit and Credit. Mother-Love. The Keys of Heaven.

1897-1912. Toward Damascus, I-III.

Advent. There Are Crimes and Crimes. The Saga of the Folkungs. Gustavus Vasa. Eric XIV. Gustavus Adolphus. Midsummer. Easter. The Dance of Death, I and II. Engelbrecht. Charles XII. The Crown Bride. Swanwhite. The Dream Play. Queen Christina. Gustavus III. The Nightingale of Wittenberg. Storm. The Fire Ruins. The Spook Sonata. The Pelican. The Black Glove. Earl Birger. The National Director. The Last Knight. The Slippers of Abu Casem. The Great Highway.

Novels and Stories

1869-85. Spring Time. The Red Room. Swedish Events and Adventures, I and II. Marriage, I. Real Utopias.

1886-96. Marriage, II. The People at Hemsö. Fisher Folks. Chandalah. The Island of the Blessed. At the Edge of the Sea. Fables.

1897-1912. Sagas. The Gothic Rooms.

Historical Miniatures. New Swedish Adventures. Black Flags. The Scapegoat.

AUTOBIOGRAPHICAL FICTION

1869-85. He and She. Going Home to Be Tried.

1886-96. The Bondwoman's Son. When the Sap Is Stirring. In the Red Room. The Author. A Fool's Confession.

1897-1912. Inferno. Legends. Fairhaven and Foulstrand. Alone.

VERSE

1869-85. Poems. Somnambulistic Day-Dreams.

1897-1912. Word-Play.

HISTORICAL AND SCIENTIFIC WORKS

1869-85. Studies of Civilization. The Swedish People in War and Peace.

1886-96. Among French Peasants. On

120 VOICES OF TO-MORROW

the Relations Between France and Sweden. Jardin des plantes. Antibarbarus. Types and Prototypes.

1897-1912. The Conscious Will Revealed in History. A Free Norway. The Origins of the Swedish Language. Biblical Proper Names. The Roots of the Great Languages. China and Japan. The Democratic State.

Essays, Criticism, Etc.

1869-85. The New Kingdom. A Little of Everything. From Italy.

1886-96. Little Studies of Plants and Animals. Pieces Printed and Unprinted, I and II.

1897-1912. The Blue Books, I-III. Letters and Memoranda to the Members of the Intimate Theatre; two pamphlets. Studies of Shakespeare's Dramas; three pamphlets. Speeches to the Swedish Nation. Religious Renascence.

BJÖRNSTJERNE BJÖRNSON

Poet, Politician, Prophet

SOME writers, like Ibsen, seem to disappear behind their own work. With Björnstjerne Björnson it was different. In his case the man tended constantly to obscure the work. The reason lies near at hand. Ibsen, for instance, concentrated all his efforts toward a single point of attack— the modern drama. Björnson, on the other hand, aimed always at covering the whole front line of human progress. Wherever he saw the spirit of man struggling to rise above its present level, there he must needs give help. In doing so he used his art frankly as a means to an end. The wonder of it is that Björnson nevertheless proved himself a great and exquisite artist.

In some quarters, especially Scandinavian, it was long the fashion to praise his poetry while regretting—or even reviling—his activity as reformer, patriot and moralist. Yet this meant a denial of all that Björnson really stood for. And it implied a condemnation of his art as well, if this is seen in the light I have just suggested. For he was first of all a teacher and fighter and prophet—not a shaper of beautiful forms. To him the form was always subordinate to the spirit, art to life. What actuated his whole being, coloring his written and spoken words, his public actions and private life, was his passion for truth, for cleanliness of soul, for the binding of man to man by ties of love instead of force. For this faith he fought untiringly during sixty years. At the same time he placed his whole mighty personality, with all its splendid gifts, against every form of oppression, whether exercised upon individuals, classes, or entire nations.

Though the son of a country minister, he sprang from a long line of peasant forefathers. In the heart of the real country, among the peasants, he was born and reared. And throughout his long life he never broke that once established contact with nature and the mass of common men. In later years it made him buy a big farm in the very heart of the Norwegian uplands. Not only did he make Aulestad, as he called it, his true home, but he found time to turn it into a model farm in order that his countrymen might profit by his example.

To his ancestry and upbringing must be traced his unswerving, life-long faith in modern democracy. To the same origin may also be attributed a vitality that seemed inexhaustible and that made his antipathies as well as his sympathies nearly irresistible. To come near him, or even to read his printed words, sufficed to make one conscious of the wonderful power that emanated from him and that drew other men to him as the magnet draws the steel. A friend said of him once that "there was not an undeveloped muscle in his body nor an unused cell in his brain." This physical and mental wholesomeness went far to explain the intensity of his passion for purity in the highest sense of that word.

From first to last his spirit showed a spontaneity and freshness of sympathy and interest that kept him youthful up to the very moment when the first forewarning of approaching death reached him. He was ever seeking new truths to master and new causes to champion. In this search he was invariably guided by what he deemed right, not by what the world held expedient. As he was in great things, so he was in small ones—a big child, with a warm heart and a keen mind. He was already full of years and fame when he told a friend that the possession of a new pair of trousers made him get up an hour ahead of time in order that he might get that much more enjoyment out of putting them on for the first time. One Christmas when, in accordance with ancient custom, melted tallow had been sprinkled on the ground for the titmice to feast on, his wife saw him sitting in a very uncomfortable position near one of the windows of his study.

"Why," he cried in response to her question, "I have to watch the sparrows, of course, or they will steal the tallow away from the titmice."

That was the man of whom a friend said that "he risked his reputation at least once a year for some cause he believed in." It was the same man, too, who wrote to Zola while a majority of the French people were condemning them both for their defense of Dreyfus: "The relation of a poet to his works should be like that of a bank to the currency it issues—there must be plenty of good securities in the vaults."

One day in the early fifties he startled the Norwegian capital by appearing at the only theatre as the leader of 600 youths armed with whistles. The storm that followed ended the sway of Danish acting and Danish language on the Norwegian stage. Thus he entered upon his lifework of reestablishing the national spirit of his country on a higher and more genuine level. In that long struggle, which exposed him to so much hatred both at home and abroad, his cry was not "My country, right or wrong," but always, "Norway must do right at any cost!" For this reason he never deserved the name of politician, as this has generally been applied in the past. But he accepted it gladly, declaring that politics should be to the social body what morals are to the individual.

It was during those first, feverishly active years that he wrote his peasant stories and thus made Norwegian poetry appreciated beyond its native boundaries. While those firstlings of his pen have at times been unduly exalted at the expense of his riper work, one must grant them an originality and a charm that secure them a place entirely by themselves. Such stories as "Synnöve Solbakken," "Arne," and "A Happy Boy" have perhaps a wider appeal than anything else Björnson wrote. Nor is the interest attaching to them merely artistic. In building them—as well as the first plays, dating from the same period—he applied truly historic methods to art. According to his own assertion, he reached his results "by viewing the peasant in the light of the old Sagas, and the Sagas in the light of modern peasant life."

To consider what Björnson tried to do and actually did during the fifties and sixties is like looking into a fairy world, unaffected by ordinary human limitations. There was not a movement afoot in which he did not take part for or against. There was not a public question raised that he did not have to discuss in speech and writing. He was newspaper editor and contributor, theatrical director and playwright, political agitator and leader, poet and novelist—all at the same time and in bewildering alternation. A mere youth, he did more than most to build that radical party of the Left, which has now shaped the destinies of Norway for more than a quarter-century. Through his patriotic poems he stirred the national spirit as it had never been stirred before, and one of those poems—"Yes, We Love the Land that Bore Us"—took such hold of the people that, in a very few years, it became the national hymn.

In the seventies his life took on a new aspect. He travelled and wrote. Secret, silent forces were at work within him. In quick succession he produced eight modern plays, each one of which struck to the heart of some vital question then uppermost in the mind of the public. In "The Editor" he dealt not so much with the press as with the kind of men that were frequently in control of it in those days—self-seeking freebooters without any sense of social responsibility. "A Business Failure" and "The New System" attacked and exposed the commercial spirit, the passion for speculation and unearned gains, the falseness and shallowness of so-called "social" life. In "The King" he pictured the blighting effect of the monarchical convention not upon the people but upon the monarch himself.

But none of these dramas of modern life created such a sensation—not only in Norway but all through the Western world—as "A Gauntlet," in which Björnson dared to deny the need of a double standard of sexual morality for men and women. In some ways the powerful woman movement in the Scandinavian countries may be dated back to that one play, with its inexorable demand, not that both sexes have equal right to live as they please, but that both have equal duty to keep themselves pure in body and spirit. To few other questions has Björnson returned so frequently and with so much fervor as to this one. He dealt with it again in his two great novels, "The House of the Kurts" and "In God's Ways." He made it the subject of a lecture on "Monogamy or Polygamy," which, in 1887, he delivered in more than sixty different places within the three Scandinavian countries and Finland. And it enters into almost everything else he has ever written.

That nature may require man to live a

different life from woman's he would never admit. And he insisted on tracing much of what is evil, both in the existence of the individual and of the race, to false sexual ideals and relationships. On the other hand, he kept himself free from the prudishness generally displayed by advocates of similar opinions in other countries. Love was to him always the great moving power of the world, and he could imagine no love more beautiful or compelling than that which draws the right man to the right woman and holds both together in a union for life.

With his criticism of the traditional male attitude in sex matters, Björnson combined from the first a demand that women be given full economical, social, and political equality with men. This he did not only out of a sense of abstract justice but also because, like Ibsen and Auguste Comte, he believed that the future of the race rested largely with the classes hitherto kept away from public affairs—that is, with women and workmen. Step by step he brought his countrymen round to his own viewpoint in this matter, and to-day Norway stands in this respect practically where Björnson would have it; the rights and duties of man are also the rights and duties of woman, and no class is excluded from full participation in the government.

All his life Björnson was deeply religious. During his earlier years he found in Christianity a satisfactory expression for this phase of his being. And it was with sincere sorrow that he saw Ibsen taking a more and more negative attitude toward the accepted creed of his country. In the seventies, however, Björnson passed through a crisis, as I have already told. The concrete truths of modern science claimed his attention to an increasing extent. He read Darwin, Spencer and Mill. Little by little the old faith fell away from him. The reflections of that period appear in the charming novel named "Dust." But though the dogmas of Christianity lost their meaning for him, his spirit retained its essentially religious quality. In no work is this more clearly evidenced than in the first part of his great double play, "Beyond Our Power." Next to the peasant stories it is probably the work best known in the English-speaking countries. Here, as on the other side, it has been much misunderstood. That it offers chances for contradictory constructions cannot be denied. But read in conjunction with the second part—written after an interval of twelve years and dealing with modern social conditions—it seems to tell man that his faith cannot be placed with safety on the miracles promised either by religious or social extremists.

It was in the eighties—after a prolonged visit to the United States, where he exercised a powerful influence on the numerous Scandinavians in the West, and where he also developed a passionate admiration for Lincoln—that Björnson earned his nickname of "Norway's uncrowned king." Rarely in human history has the life of a people been to such an extent focused in the life of a single individual, who yet was merely a private citizen. While determined that Norway should have no foreign guardianship, Björnson was at no time moved by hostility to Sweden or any other nation. Behind his fervent nationalism lay a no less fervent hope for a united Scandinavia; but the union, he felt, must be voluntary and based on complete equality. Here, as always, the fundamental motive was his faith in modern democracy. And even in those days he was already cherishing the still vaster dream of a great Pan-Germanic federation, rooted not in conquest or in the suppression of the smaller nationalities, but in free cooperation and common cultural interests.

The "clean flag," without the customary union mark at the upper corner, was the symbol he selected for his new Norway. For this symbol he fought against one-half of his own nation and all Sweden. At the same time he declared openly that he wanted "to dissolve the union in the minds of the people," and how well he did that work was shown in 1905. But he insisted on peaceful methods, respect for the rights of the other side, and postponement of final action until all Norwegian parties could agree on a common program. The irony of fate would have it that when the deciding crisis arrived at last he could take no part. He disapproved of the methods chosen for the breaking of the union. Once the break had occurred, however, he turned around in eager defense of his people before the rest of the world. As on many previous occasions, he achieved this through a series of brilliant articles and letters contributed to the leading European newspapers and periodicals. They used to say while Norway had not yet a diplomatic service of its own, that such an institution was not needed as long as Björnson represented the country abroad.

What occupied his mind more than anything else during the last period of his life was probably the idea of universal peace with its attendant substitution of arbitration for war. To him it seemed clear that such an idea could never become materialized except through the reformation of all international and inter-racial relationships on a basis of mutual sympathy and justice. He demanded national cleanliness and righteousness as he had formerly demanded those virtues of the individual. In the pursuit of these new ideals he became the fearless champion of all human groups held in forced subjugation to some stronger group. Time and again he took up the pen on behalf of the Finlanders against Russia, of the Slovaks against Hungary, of the Danes and the Poles against Prussia. Nothing could better prove his sincerity and courage than that his defense of these suffering nationalities was undertaken at a time when his own country was still greatly in need of the moral support of the powers he attacked.

His last years were rendered singularly happy by the growing comprehension of his spirit everywhere. His visit to Paris in

1901 was more triumphant in some respects than that of a crowned monarch. The celebration of his seventieth birthday anniversary in 1902 engaged the attention of the whole civilized world. In 1903 he was given the Nobel prize for literature, and acknowledged the honor in a remarkable address on "poetry as a manifestation of the sense of vital surplus." What he was to his own people is best made clear by an incident which occurred at his beloved Aulestad not long before he was forced to start on his final journey to Paris in vain search of another lease of health and life. A regiment passed the place in the course of a manœuvre. Its commander sent word ahead to the poet asking him to review the soldiers as they marched by. Björnson stood on the veranda of his house, surrounded by his entire family—a man who had never held any public office, mind you! As the troop approached on the highroad below, officers and men gave the salute due to a commanding general or a member of the royal house.

But this was not all. From the rapidly moving ranks rose one mighty shout after another—a spontaneous outburst of devotion and gratitude such as it has been granted very few men the fortune to inspire.

Björnson was nearly seventy-seven years old when, in 1909, he brought out a new play—his last finished work—which was given with surprising success in the Scandinavian countries and Germany. Among other works from that final period, when the poet had already crossed the supposed boundary line of creative power, may be mentioned the charming novel "Mary" and not less than four plays: "Paul Lange and Tora Parsberg," "Laboremus," "At Storhove," and "Dayland." In several of these he took sharp issue against the exaggerated individualism which had fed on Nietzsche and which seemed particularly to attract the youth all over the world.

When at last the message came that the man who so long had seemed invincible was about to be conquered by death, a hush fell over all Scandinavia. For the first time in years, Norwegians, Swedes and Danes forgot their perennial bickerings in a united outpouring of apprehension and sorrow. Everybody saw suddenly in the dying poet the principal embodiment of their kinship and their common cultural heritage. He who, in the prime of his manhood, had so often been accused of sowing strife and misunderstanding, was now recognized as the man who had bidden each people "to be itself in truth" in order that it might more fully win the respect and confidence of all the others.

The news of his death, which took place at Paris in April, 1910, was everywhere received with a conviction that his passing implied the loss of a great heart, capable of embracing the whole world in its love, and of a poet whose purpose was identical with the triumphant progress of all humanity.

THE STORY OF SELMA LAGERLÖF

SELMA LAGERLÖF is one of the greatest of an increasing group of writers who represent a synthesis of two past literary epochs, and who, for this reason, must be held especially representative of the literary epoch that is now coming. She has revived not only the courage but the ability to feel and dream and aspire that belonged to the scorned romanticists of the early nineteenth century. But this recovery of something long held to be lost and outlived forever she has achieved for us without surrender of that intimate connection between poetry and real life which was established by the naturalists in the latter half of the same century. The romanticists spoke to our hearts alone. The naturalists spoke only to our heads. For the men and women of the new epoch we have not yet found an adequate name, but we know that they are speaking to head and heart alike. We know that Selma Lagerlöf's brightest fairy raiments are woven out of what to the ordinary mind would seem like the most commonplace patches of everyday life—and we know as well that when she tempts us into far-off, fantastic worlds of her own making, her ultimate object is to help us see the inner meanings of the too often over-emphasized superficial actualities of our own existence.

"The Saga of the Making of a Saga"—such is the English equivalent of the title to a little story in which Miss Lagerlöf has described how she came to write the book that, by a single stroke, brought her a national reputation and started her on the road to international fame. That book was "Gösta Berling's Saga."

It appeared with meteoric suddenness out of the deep obscurity which surrounds any schoolteacher in a small country town. Prior to that momentous event the existence of its author had been spent in almost cloistered seclusion, far from the highways of culture and from the kind of men and events that make history and headlines in the newspapers. Of what the world calls life she had had no taste. Of what it names doing she had done nothing. Therefore, the world wondered greatly at the unforeshadowed feat, repeating anew its perennial cry: "Can anything good come out of Nazareth—or out of Landskrona?" When she produced a second book almost as good as the first one, the wonder increased. But thereafter she was accepted as one of those from whom it is natural to expect great things. Within a surprisingly short time her books and her name spread beyond her native country. And to-day, at the age of fifty-four, this unaccountable old spinster is known and loved throughout the whole Western world, not as the lucky winner of the $40,000 Nobel prize for literature (given her in 1909), but as a seldom surpassed teller of fairy tales of the rare kind that may be read with equal pleasure by children and grown-ups.

There is an inland province of Sweden called Wärmland. It is full of big forests and small lakes, of rough rocks and merry rivers, of great beauties and humble homes. It is poor in wealth, but rich in men and dreams. Out of it have come some of Sweden's finest and sweetest poets. There Selma Lagerlöf was born in an old rectory named Mårbacka, which, with all its quiet charms, she has pictured in a chapter of her first book headed "Lilliecrona's Home." She was an introspective, sickly child, and while her brothers and sisters roamed freely around the countryside, she tarried at home and listened enraptured to those innumerable tales and legends with which that province has always been alive. Out of a swarming multitude of such tales—told now by her father, now by the servants, and now

SELMA LAGERLÖF

again by some old crone drifting in for a meal—one stood out brighter, more fascinating than all the others. It was the tale of the old cavaliers that rode from manor to manor, making the whole region ring with their merry laughter and their crazy pranks. Her ears were always open to anything told, but this tale alone had a power over her heart that none other might exert.

Those tales stirred restless longings in her heart. They seemed to be calling to her, whispering to her about some great task that she was to perform some time. Gradually her vague longings shaped themselves into a passionate wish that she, herself, might become a weaver of tales to which not only silent little home-sitting girls but the whole wide world might listen. But what she never imagined was that the task waiting for her might be to retell the very tales that had grown so dear to her heart, tales that even her love looked upon as mere gossip of the countryside.

When not listening, she read; and when

not reading, she wrote. An endless stream of wild, romantic adventures flowed from her pen, each one more unreal and unoriginal than the preceding one. Her heroes represented every age but her own. They hailed from every corner of the globe but Wärmland. Most of them had lived before —in the Arabian Nights, in the Icelandic sagas, or in the romances of Walter Scott. In those days it never occurred to her that heroes not less worthy to be sung might be found much nearer to herself—even in her own memory, where dwelt those old cavaliers of Ekeby.

When not listening or reading or writing, she was "going about waiting for fortune to arrive." This fortune her dreams pictured in the form of a great publisher who was to discover by mere chance what she had written and find it so wonderful that he had to publish it. "And then," to quote her own words, "everything else would follow as a matter of course." Strange to say, that was pretty much what did happen at last, but not until many years later, when she had long ceased to wait for the fortune that seemed never to come.

At twenty-two she went to Stockholm to study at the Normal School in order that she might earn her living as a teacher. Still the dream of a writer's fame lingered within her. Still the old legends were filling her mind like so much mist, and still she was straining her eyes to glimpse the great stories she felt sure were lying beyond that mist. One day she was walking alone along one of the streets of Stockholm—a most ordinary street, without a trace of beauty or poetry to set it apart—when all of a sudden a great light blazed up within her. At the heart of that light she saw what she was to tell—saw *the tale*—saw that it was the old familiar one of the cavaliers at Ekeby—saw that it brought her heroes as luminous as any known to poetry. In that moment of vision she conceived her future mission so vividly that it made her stop right where she was. And as she stood there "the whole street rose up toward the sky and sank down again, rose up and sank down." And when she returned to reality once more, she must needs look around with blushing cheeks and her mind wondering whether, perchance, others had also seen what she saw, or whether they had merely seen the foolish way in which she was behaving.

She did not enter at once upon the task she knew now to be hers, for while she had discovered what she had to tell, she had not yet learned how she was to tell it. Years of hard study and hard labor for a living passed by before more light came. She tried and tried—and mostly in the manner of the day. Remember that it was the day of naturalism, of photography, of preoccupation with surface appearances. How could fairy tales—even though they were real—be told in the manner of such a day? So she strove in vain, her material and her form refusing obstinately to meet in that harmony which makes a real story. She tried verse and she tried to wield the old

SELMA LAGERLÖF 147

tale into a drama. "No, no, no!" it cried—and there she was, until one day word reached her that her old parental home was to be sold.

She journeyed in haste to have one more sight of it before it ceased to be a home—and there, in her childhood surroundings, the final inspiration came to her. The spirit of romanticism which had lain dead and buried so many years came to life again and took up its abode in her soul, filling it with a new insight and a new courage. Then and there she vowed to tell the old tale in her own way, humbly but without fear, letting it come just as it would choose to come. On her return to the little city in southern Sweden where she was teaching school she sketched out three chapters in so many nights, "the pages filling themselves with a quickness that she had never dreamt of." After that the week-day cares of her profession closed in upon her again, and again a long time passed without much being done, the one difference being that now she knew both what she had to do and the way of doing it.

But at last her saga was drawing near its triumphant climax. A Swedish periodical offered a big prize for the best original novel of a hundred pages. Eight days before the closing of the contest Miss Lagerlöf decided to try for the prize with five of the chapters she had already sketched out. Two of these had assumed a form that made them immediately available, but the other three had to be practically written anew. At that time she was visiting the home of one of her sisters in the very heart of the region where the tales of the cavaliers had sprung into life. The night before the day when the manuscript must be mailed she had to attend a party. This was held in the very manor where had once lived the evil genius of the cavaliers, that old Sintram who had made a pact with the Evil One and who used to be seen travelling homeward at night after two black fire-breathing bulls. In that legend-haunted house Miss

Lagerlöf wrote the last twenty pages, sitting up all night after the party had come to an end.

The rest seems almost dull in comparison with what has been told so far. She was awarded the prize, as we all know—and this, although the work she submitted was merely a torso. To complete it became then an imperative necessity, and friends arranged things so that she could take a year's leave of absence for that purpose. And in 1891 "Gösta Berling's Saga" reached the public in the shape with which we are now familiar.

Once she had begun to write in earnest, she simply had to keep on. More Wärmland tales rose out of her memory demanding to be told. Volume after volume grew out of her busy pen. In some ways they were not as good as the first one; in other ways they were even better. That initial spontaneity which gave to "Gösta Berling's Saga" a niche all by itself had been spent and could never be recovered. In its place came artistic restraint and sense of proportion in growing degrees. And on the whole, it might be said that each new book showed definite signs of advance.

After a while she left her teacher's position to give herself undividedly to writing. The late King Oscar and his youngest son, the "painter-prince," Eugene, befriended her and enabled her to realize her long cherished desire of seeing foreign lands and peoples. She won more and more admirers among small and great, among rich and poor. She bought back her beloved Mårbacka with the money her pen had earned. And—what mattered more than anything else to herself, perhaps—new tales began to reach her, tales having their roots in that vast foreign world of which she had dreamed when she tried to borrow heroes from Walter Scott and the Arabian Nights. Thus she wrote "The Miracles of Antichrist," which is laid in Sicily, and "Jesusalem," which begins in the Swedish province of Dalecarlia, her own winter

SELMA LAGERLÖF

home for many years, and ends in Palestine. The first part of the latter work proved a tale even greater than that which she had woven around the wayward figure of Gösta Berling. Its first and final chapters are counted among the finest things our latter-day literature has to offer.

Long before this second masterpiece of hers placed her fame on a solid basis, it had spread to other countries than her own, and as a rule she was received as one carrying precious gifts. Not so in this country, however, when her three first volumes were brought out here. A few knowing ones read and gave thanks and passed on the good word: that once more it had pleased the gods of song and saga to bless the earth with a true poet. But the mass remained indifferent. Soon copies of those three volumes might be had for a few cents from among the deadwood littering the stalls outside the second-hand bookstores, which is the customary sign of commercial failure in the land of letters. When "Jerusalem" was ready, the firm that had already obtained the American rights deemed it wiser not to make use of them. And so it happens that, even when I am writing this, American readers remain unable to reach the book which many lovers of Miss Lagerlöf's art consider her greatest.

But nevertheless she was to conquer here also. Another firm risked the publication of that group of short stories to which she has given the name of "Christ Legends." These charming tales, at once so quaintly unreal and so startlingly real, so daringly familiar and so profoundly reverent, took the fancy of our public as decisively as the previous ones had failed to do. Finally came the book that more than any other one has made friends for her in this country—"The Adventures of Nils," both volumes of which have been charmingly translated by Mrs. Velma Swanston Howard. It is a book for children—the story of a little boy's wonderful journey through his native country and its history—but I

SELMA LAGERLÖF

have not yet found the grown-up reader of it who was unwilling to be counted a child again while the reading of it lasted. Thanks to this work, and also to the volume of short stories named "The Girl from the Marsh Croft," out of which I have taken most of the details used in re-telling Miss Lagerlöf's own story, you may now look long and hard for a cheap copy of "Gösta Berling's Saga," or "Invisible Links," or "The Miracles of Antichrist," for they have all, long ago, been snapped up and read.

THE NEW MYSTICISM

I

Its Prophet: Francis Grierson

"MEN of genius," says Francis Grierson, "are the symbols and the finger-points which nature unfolds here and there as indications of the mathematical and psychic progression of the visible and invisible world in which we live."

But that evolutionary process which we call progress presents itself to me everywhere as a pendular swinging between opposites lying now in this, now in that direction. In our efforts to determine the momentary direction of those swingings, we select, more or less arbitrarily, certain points deriving their significance from tendencies common to all life. Thus, for instance, we find it hard to indicate any kind of spiritual advance without reference to what we generally name "scepticism" and "mysticism" —principles back of which we discover fundamental attitudes of the human mind.

Surveyed from the antipodal position, scepticism appears little more than carping doubt, while mysticism, similarly viewed, implies blind faith and poor thinking. Regarded in this hostile spirit, both attitudes seem like pure negations of progress. Very differently they appear, indeed, if we study them from within, so to speak, and in proper coördination with life in its entirety. Then scepticism is seen to stand for a demand that nothing be accepted as real which cannot be tested and re-tested by our senses supported by such artificial aids as our growing ingenuity enables us to devise. And mysticism becomes then identified with an insistence on the supreme importance of realities so subtle that they lie beyond anything ascertainable by mere sense perception.

As far back as we have records of systematic thinking, we find the human mind swinging periodically between these antagonistic attitudes, the inference being that neither one of them represents the full truth, but only a part of the truth which needs temporary accentuation if life's onward course along the median line is to be maintained. We may add that the sceptical view, as a rule, draws its main inspiration from the intellect, while mysticism places the greater emphasis on the emotional side of our being.

The flowering time of classic antiquity was, on the whole, sceptical and intellectual. Christianity inaugurated an era of highly emotional mysticism that lasted up to and beyond the dawn of the Renaissance. With the beginning of what we call "modern" times, the sway passed to reason, and up to the eve of the French Revolution man's spirit continued to grow more and more dryly sceptical. The nearer we come to our own day, the shorter and quicker grow the swingings of the pendulum. The emotional period named the Romantic Era lasted less than a century before it yielded to another intellectual reaction, and this, again, showed signs of waning within a few decades. The characteristic mark of this most recent period of scepticism was that it discouraged any venturing beyond that central field of obvious existence on which falls the full light of our self-consciousness. And our main reasons for feeling that our faces are once more set toward the mystical pole lie in the eagerness with which we are now shedding our former agnostic timidity, and in the growing tendency to spend at least a small part of ourselves in those marginal tracts of being upon which falls the shadow of the unknowable.

When, in 1886, Ibsen published "Rosmersholm," the end of naturalism in literature and of materialism in philosophy was already in sight. Three years later a single twelvemonth encompassed three outwardly unrelated events, each one of which must be held momentous in the annals of the present spiritual phase. In 1889 Maeterlinck published his first play, "Princess Maleine." In 1889 Bergson sent forth his first great philosophical work, which has only recently become familiar in this country under its English title of "Time and Free Will." And in that same year a tiny volume of essays and aphorisms in French was printed privately at Paris by Francis Grierson under the name of "La Révolte Idéaliste."

Within certain circles that little volume was hailed as a revelation and a battle cry. Maeterlinck read it and expressed his admiration openly. The general public heard no more of it than of Bergson's coëval work. Of course, the early plays of Maeterlinck warned many of an impending change. And in each new drama turned out by Ibsen toward the end of his life, the mystical tendency asserted itself more strongly. But I think that the first book which made the beginning of a new period palpably evident was "The Treasure of the Humble," appearing in 1896. In the same year Bergson published his second volume, named "Matter and Memory." And three years later Grierson issued his first book in English— a group of essays bearing the significant title of "Modern Mysticism" and including much of what had already been printed in the earlier French volume.

Life has a way of making many tools work as one, while each of them thinks itself alone "on the job." This is practically what happened to the three men in whom I am inclined to see living pillars of the thought-structure most expressive of our own day and its tendencies. Each one of them may owe something to the other two, and yet all of them were from the start impelled by a common spirit and would probably in the end have reached a clear understanding of this spirit without mutual assistance. Maeterlinck has proved himself more of an artist than Grierson, and Bergson more of a thinker. The formulations of both Maeterlinck and Bergson are more definite in outline than those of Grierson. But to Grierson belongs the honor of having first attained to prophetic vision of the common goal. For that humble volume of 1889 suggested more or less gropingly every idea which since then has become recognized as essential, not only to Maeterlinck and Bergson, but to the constantly increasing number of writers who are now engaged in making the time conscious of its own spirit. And it is as one of nature's "finger-points"—the first one of its kind to bear a fairly plain inscription— that Grierson interests me.

His position in the van of modern thought is the more remarkable because he began life as a musician, and under circumstances that, at first glance, would seem decidedly unfavorable to his later literary development. It is doubtful, however, whether he could ever have become what we now see in him without just the kind of experience that filled his earlier years. Born at Birkenhead, England, in 1848, he was over

FRANCIS GRIERSON 161

forty when he issued his first book, and over fifty when he began to gain widespread recognition as a writer. In connection with his strongly individualistic attitude and his impatient scorn of what he calls "provincialism," it is interesting to note that one of his ancestors was that Sir Robert Grierson, fourteenth Laird of Lagg, who figures so conspicuously in Scott's "Redgauntlet."

When the boy was only a year old, his parents emigrated to this country. After several westward moves, the family settled at last in the prairie country of southern Illinois, where abolitionism was then assuming its first practical expression through the "underground railway," and where a little later Lincoln began his struggle for national leadership. The time was already big with the coming crisis. Men's minds were strangely restless and expectant. A wave of mingled religious and political emotion was sweeping the country. The old prophecies were chanted with a new meaning. When not wholly overlooked, the little everyday things became symbolical of life-embracing truths. And as in most periods of great tension, the people shunned the sceptical spirit ordinarily glorified under the name of "common sense."

That earliest environment stamped itself on the supersensitive boy for life. The wind-swept vastness of the prairie filled his soul with a wonder that is still stirring mightily within the man of sixty-five. He attended some of those cyclonic revivals that prostrated whole counties in common awe and faith. He watched the mysterious arrivals and departures of frightened, chattering fugitives. He heard Lincoln and Douglas debate, and, a mere boy, he even took a minor part in the tumult that ensued when at last the pent-up passions of incompatible civilizations clashed openly.

Through all those disturbing impressions flowed influences of a more intimate character that, fortunately, made for mental poise and a calm faith in the powers within.

Like shining, winged guardians, the memories of his father's quiet nobility and his mother's patient kindliness have always remained with him, making him kind and considerate toward everybody, patient and dignified in the face of everything. Nor is he able to hark back to a moment when everything that was most himself did not leap in mysterious response to the sound of his mother's voice—a voice peculiarly sonorous and sweet even when she spoke, but trembling with almost unearthly harmonies when she raised it in song. From his mother must have emanated the gift which later brought him an all but unique place in the world of music.

In 1863 the family moved east again. And in 1868 Grierson was at Washington, meeting Walt Whitman and practicing the art peculiarly his own. I don't know when or how he discovered his ability to improvise on the piano a music always comparable to, and sometimes surpassing, the best composed in the ordinary manner. All I know is that when, in 1869, he made his European début at Paris, he won the startled approbation of the most critical audiences in the world. And for years that tall boy of Byronic appearance, who could not even read music from the sheet, and who seems to have had little or no systematic instruction, went triumphantly from country to country, gaining everywhere the hearing and favor of the great ones, whether crowned or laurelled. To this day Grierson's command of the piano remains as perfect and as inexplicable as ever.

Persons of sound judgment, who have heard him, say that his playing has an indescribable quality, found in none that is studied from the sheet and developed by practice. It is as if his soul were able to impress its every mood and fancy directly on the keyboard, drawing from it a music at once spontaneous and subtly expressive as that of wind and water, of reeds and trees. It is a music mirroring the strife and the prayer that accompany the human soul's struggle to solve both its own riddle and that of the encompassing universe. From the power speaking through this music Grierson may have derived the passion for spontaneous utterance and the unquestioned reliance on intuitive guidance which assert themselves so conspicuously in all his writings.

For many years Grierson moved hither and thither as the impulse of the moment prompted him. At times he took great risks, and at times he suffered hardships in consequence thereof. Mostly fate provided mysteriously for him wherever he went, causing him to believe that, for the right man at least, the thing he needs is always waiting. Frequently he found himself in company that might have proved dangerous to a mind less firmly fixed in its own spirit. It cannot be denied that he speaks eagerly, and at times a little egotistically, of his acquaintance with men and women in exalted positions. But, as a rule, he has always kept his head firm and his vision clear. And there is an unmistakable ring of truth in his words when he says that he has never yet seen the palace in which he cared to live. Concrete humanity has with him largely taken the place of books, "the idea of knowing the world from books having never entered his head." Yet he has read extensively, to good purpose, and only of what has a claim to serious attention. Now and then his critical judgments are peculiar or intolerant; in the main they are scrupulously just and eloquent of his familiarity with the best literatures of all ages.

Of the circumstances that first led him to write I know no more than of his first venture into music. As early as 1882 he delivered some discourses on "Materialism in Germany" and "The Influence of Modern Literature from a Spiritual Standpoint," which were published—but when and how I cannot tell. The essays and aphorisms forming his first volume he seems to have produced for his own pleasure alone and with no thought of giving them to the public. This he did only with hesitation and at the urgent requests of his friend, L. Waldemar Tonner, who has been his constant companion for more than twenty-five years. The reception given that initial volume was, as I have already mentioned, flattering enough as far as it went, but it did very little to bring its author before the general public. The main thing it did for him was to reveal his true field of endeavor.

It seems likely that Grierson was not unmindful of his own case when he wrote that "all men and women are heroic who have worked, waited and suffered without losing faith in themselves." He has always been a master in the art of waiting, and his faith in the ultimate success of his work seems never to have wavered. Ten years passed before he produced his second book, in English, and even then it was largely made up of what had already entered into the previous volume. It was that book of essays named "Modern Mysticism," which still may be counted Grierson's chief personal message to mankind. Two years later, in 1901, he published another group of essays and reflections under the title of "The Celtic Temperament." Both these works aroused a great deal of attention in England, and had he continued without interruption to produce books of the same kind, his reputation might have spread more rapidly among the public at large.

Instead he took up a long-cherished project of giving artistic form to his childhood reminiscences of Lincoln's time and country. It was a work of love on which he spent eight years and all his savings. He named the book "The Valley of Shadows" when it appeared in 1909. It is in every way a remarkable production, not known as it deserves on this side of the ocean. It is the one work of Grierson's in which the form equals the contents and the spirit in importance. Perfection cannot be claimed for it. As much of what has sprung from Grierson's pen, it is weak in design, containing whole chapters not germane to its purpose. But it makes us live once more in the physical and spiritual atmosphere of its chosen time and place. Its pages haunt us with their strange mingling of exquisite art and artless simplicity. To read that book and remain the same man as before seems out of the question. Judging it as a piece of art, this work ranks far ahead of anything else Grierson has done hitherto. Nevertheless I shall not recur to it again because, after all, I do not think it bears the same vital relation to the spirit and outlook of the time as do his essays.

Since the appearance of "The Valley of Shadows," Grierson has given us a volume of reminiscent essays named "Parisian Portraits," another volume of literary and philosophical essays called "The Humor of the Underman," and a volume of essays and aphorisms in French, "La Vie et les Hommes." These later works offer few ideas not present in the earlier ones, but they are valuable for the additional light they throw on Grierson's life view, besides being richly endowed with the charm attaching to all he has written.

Even at this late date Grierson remains, on the whole, a "writer's writer"—one appealing to the few rather than to the many. To this exclusiveness he would be the last one to raise any objection, for toward the mass of men his attitude has always been a little impatient, and it is difficult for him to approach life except from the viewpoint which Tarde designated as the "inventor's." In spite of this reserve inherent in his work, something like a Grierson cult has, during the last few years, begun to gather adherents on both sides of the ocean. This I mention merely as evidence of the close connection between Grierson's thought and the tendencies by which the race-mind is most affected for the moment.

It is with the spirit rather than the form of Grierson's work I am concerned in this study. Yet his form is not a negligible factor if we want to arrive at a correct estimate of his achievement. He himself is a worshipper of beauty in all its embodiments, and his conception of the part it plays in the general scheme of life is suggested by his saying that, "as a dance without harmonious movement has no charm, so an idea without style has no force." His style is often exquisite and always effective. In his striving after perfect form, however, he is more English than French, paying more attention to expression than to design, which seems strange in one who places such stress on brevity and directness, and who has given us what almost amounts to a new literary category, standing between the essay and the aphorism.

His thoughts leap rather than flow, and at times he passes from one to another with an abruptness that both startles and puzzles the reader. The same abruptness seems characteristic of most writers who are what might be called intellectually self-made. It implies at bottom a contempt for those smooth commonplaces which we are so prone to use in passing from one link to another in our chain of argument. What, on the other hand, may justly be deemed a defect lies in the tendency of Grierson to lapse into hopeless confusion whenever he attempts a categorical subdivision of any general group of phenomena. Then, more than at any other time, he proves himself a writer and thinker to whom rigid classification and systematization are essentially foreign.

Whoever sees in pigeon-holed comprehensiveness the chief desideratum had better not seek it in Grierson's pages. There he will find no logically arranged system, no creed neatly done up in "fourthlies" and "fifthlies," while ever so often he will discover indisputable evidences of self-contradiction. But Grierson neither is nor pretends to be a philosopher in the academic sense. He has as much passion as Bergson, if not more, for keeping his conception of life fluid. And he writes, not for pedants, but for brave and tolerant temperaments, ready to forgive verbal inconsistencies if only the spirit be consistent, and eager to use the ideas offered them as bricks for the upbuilding of their own systems. If approached in the right way, he will always be found suggestive, though never exhaustive in any sense. Purposely obscure he is not, but sometimes his thoughts are a little too far-reaching for the ordinary run of words, and therefrom results a certain vagueness calling for sympathetic cooperation on the part of the reader. And of one thing such a reader may always be sure: that back of every blurred passage will be felt the pressure of mystic meanings, heralding what to later generations may appear as plain, familiar truths.

Of course, it is inevitable that one who has brooded so insistently on all the riddles that make up our existence, as well as on some that seem to reach beyond it, must have arrived at certain formulations that meet us with an air of conclusiveness. But interesting as these may be in themselves, they are not what makes Grierson's work valuable to us. The basis of that value lies in something much subtler, something almost defying our efforts at definition. More than anything else it resembles a mood, an attitude, but one so consistent and so enduring that it constitutes the equivalent of a logical life interpretation. It is as if Grierson *felt* rather than *saw* what life implies in its utmost ramifications and consequences, and as if, from this feeling amounting almost to vision, he had derived a golden rule as to the way life should be lived under any and every circumstance.

Of this attitude he is wont to speak in certain constantly recurring terms, which vary with the point of approach. When he deals with valuations of life, he is likely to use words like "pessimism" and "disillusionment." When, again, he considers the methods of effective living, he employs such terms as "intuition," "imagination," and "inspiration." With his pessimism we need not concern ourselves at length. Its quality is provokingly evasive, and Grierson's meaning might be equally clear if he used the antithetical term of optimism. He does, in fact, play ball with those two terms, choosing now one and now the other to represent the same thing, or making one of them by turns express quite different things. But what he is really aiming at one rarely fails to catch. In the end it amounts to this: that he sees life as a striving and not as a holding—as a journey and not as an arrival. To him the fatuous optimism of the early eighteenth century, for instance, means nothing but a belief that some day life will reach a final equilibrium; while that "modern melancholy," with its "natural gesture of disillusionment," to which he sometimes refers as "practical pessimism," means a realization, on the part both of the individual and the race, that eternal disharmony is the price which must be paid for eternal progress.

"Men are potent and persevering from fear of the future," he says, "and never from an absolute confidence in it." With despair or resigned inactivity, with all the repellent features of that surrender which makes for decadence in art as in life, his peculiar brand of pessimism has absolutely nothing in common. Of such decadent, life-destroying pessimism he says that those given to it "take the trivial and fleeting things of life as if they were intended to remain as perpetual realities instead of passing incidents." Perhaps his own feeling in this matter comes nearest authentic manifestation in a passage where he says that "in everything development mounts upward by regular stages, the last expression in the ladder of progress being the most favorable, but never final." This is modern, vitalistic evolutionism, with its placing of perfectional striving, not achieved perfection, at the heart of life. And it is in thorough keeping with the spirit common to men like Ostwald and Mach, Bergson and Cope, that Grierson adds: "For we shall not reach finality till the last flicker of hope goes out on the shores of Silence and Eternity."

But still nearer to Grierson's life conception do we come when we turn to that other set of terms which he is wont to use—the terms indicative of what to him appears the proper method of dealing with life's problems. And it follows, of course, from what was said above, that to him life primarily must present itself as an endless series of problems demanding solution. Both his preoccupation with methods of living and his instinctive clinging to the aphoristic form in writing as well as thinking, confirms our impression of him as a preacher and prophet rather than philosopher—one more anxious to tell us how to live than what life is. What he wants to give and has to give in richest measure may be expressed in a single word: wisdom. As we read essay after essay, it is as if we beheld the globe of life revolving slowly between us and some unknown source of light, the rays of which lend an edge of transparency to the core of opaqueness.

Grierson's books fall naturally into the class of "Ecclesiastes," for which he has such fondness; and it is only logical that he should judge the worth of an author by the number of life-enlightening phrases to be culled from his work. The wisdom that finds expression in his own pithy and polished phrases has a quaint streak of worldly shrewdness running through its essential unworldliness, showing that wherever his head be, his feet are always on firm ground. This element of homely common sense may have been acquired while he received the intoxicating homage reserved for a musical prodigy, or it may be traceable to his impressions of those canny Illinois settlers, who retained a certain balance even in the midst of religious excesses. No matter where he got it, we may be glad he does possess it, for just this mixture of two widely different kinds of wisdom tends to give his mysticism the quality which renders it suitable to the mood of our own day.

Too often in the past mysticism has prided itself on being fantastic and impractical. Too often it has stood wholly hostile to that light of "cold reason" which Blake declared to be "the only enemy of God." But we of to-day feel differently, and we are not willing to sacrifice what the painstaking intellectual labors of the last few centuries have gained for us. We want to arrive at a more correct estimate of the power and scope of our intellectual faculty, but we do not wish to abolish it—supposing this to be possible. What we aim at is a blending of emotion and intellect from which will spring a still higher faculty, capable of reaching closer to life's utmost confines and innermost recesses than either one of its constituent parts. It is because this desire of ours is so completely Grierson's that he takes such eminent rank among those who are now leading mankind on to a never before attained degree of self-consciousness.

For however strenuously he may harp on the saving grace of that quality which, by turns, he speaks of as intuition, imagination and inspiration, he maintains no less strenuously that this voice out of our subconscious depths must be checked by scientific interpretation. In other words, it is some synthesis like the one just indicated, and not another form of onesidedness, for which he pleads. He has said, I admit, that "the longer he lives, the less he esteems work that is purely intellectual." But he has also said that "the world is not governed by what bodies of people do or say, but by ideas." And, although he asserts that "profound feeling is one of the principal ingredients of genius," he has made clear in numerous passages that sentimentalism and unbridled emotionalism are as foreign to him as occultism and any kind of supernaturalism.

When he tells us to heed the voice of

intuition, or insists that "imagination is the basic pillar of science as well as romance," he wants us to turn our vision inward and not backward. He wants us not to abandon our search for truth, but to search for it in a direction long neglected and discredited. It is one of the chief traits of our own day that it has begun to grasp the part played by emotion in our dealings with the hard task of comprehending life. And to this grasp our present mystical trend must be largely traced. We are beginning to see that our intellectual consciousness, from which springs scepticism and its entire groundwork of inductive reasoning, always tends to run into a sharp point and end there. All such consciousness may be likened to an angle turned upward: beyond its apex there is nothing. Mysticism, on the other hand, and also deductive reasoning, may be represented by an angle standing on its apex and opening outward until all life may be included within its embrace. Each one of those conscious forms has its warrant and its use. What we want is to combine them—to join those two angles so that where they meet we get a focal point toward which converges all the past, all reality that has already been conquered, and from which diverges the whole future with its infinity of still unmeasured realities.

To me emotion is a general reaction of the whole system, that juxtaposes itself, on one side, to the peripheral reactions of the senses, and on the other, to the centralized reactions of the brain. Instinct is emotion turning into action without interference of the reason. Intuition, according to Bergson, is instinct grown self-conscious. And imagination, as I see it, is intellect impelled by intuition—or, if it please you better, plunged into the deep recesses of subconscious being and thus brought into more direct communication with that source of life which is also the ultimate source of all knowledge.

Mysticism has always demanded a plunge of some such kind, but the distinguishing mark of our new mysticism is that the plunge stands neither for an end in itself nor for a negation of the ordinary modes and objects of consciousness. The mystic of to-day does not dream of extinguishing the searchlight of self-consciousness. He wishes only to reverse it, in order that by its light he may explore the world within and thus attain to new sympathy and new understanding for the world without. He is not renouncing knowledge based on the testimony of the senses and the judgment of the brain: he is instead trying to supplement it with knowledge reached by new routes. These routes have too long been rejected by the spirit of scepticism, of mechanical rationalism, of one-sided materialism, that was needed to teach us once for all what is knowledge and what is not. To the new mystic—as we find him embodied in Grierson, for instance—the heart has its own wireless system, and this he wants us to study with all the keenness of which the head is capable, so that thereby the hand may gain added precision in its moulding of what Ibsen called "the third kingdom" and Grierson somewhere speaks of as "the precincts of perpetual magic."

As seen by Grierson, the world is full of mysterious coincidences, of secretly ordained and regulated happenings, of signs and symbols with almost cabalistic portent. But these manifestations of a world not yet subdued by our senses imply nothing occult, nothing that may not be held strictly "natural." Beneath the perishable surface he spies an imperishable and immanent life principle, to which he may or may not give the name of God, as the mood of the moment happens to connect his dreams with the past or with the future. His creed, largely unformulated, is at bottom nothing but that ancient pantheism, that primal glimmer of truth, which has haunted man's mind ever since he began to make gods in his own image, and which will continue to haunt him until he surrenders to its wise promptings and recognizes the whole world and all life as divine. With this in mind, Grierson defines our own epoch, the twentieth century, as the one in which "science is at last to coalesce with the pantheistic idea of the Greeks." Science must be there as one of the fusing principles; it stands for reason, for the scepticism of the test tube and the scales. But reason is no longer to be the sole witness bearing testimony: beside it will be heard intuition—the voice of life itself rising through our emotions into the steady, dispassionate light of the intellect.

II

Its Poet: Maurice Maeterlinck

WHEN, in 1911, it became known that the Belgian poet-philosopher had been awarded the Nobel prize for literature, none of the usual clamorous dissent was heard—nothing, in fact, but pleased approval. Back of this rare accord between the much-criticized Swedish Academy and an irreverent world might lie nothing but admiration granted by our reasons to one who has moulded the unborn thoughts of his time into lucid and melodious words. But I am inclined to seek for a more potent explanation, and to find it in a feeling so strong and intimate that it can be described only as love. And this much, it seems to me, is universally given to Maeterlinck, not

MAURICE MAETERLINCK

as a poet and thinker alone, but as a personality—as a beacon soul, at once pure and strong, wise and sweet, toward which our hearts instinctively turn in their search for consolation and inspiration.

There was a time, not so very long ago, when, to use James Huneker's striking phrase, "Maeterlinck meant for most people a crazy crow masquerading in tail feathers plucked from the Swan of Avon." As he stands before us to-day, modern literature knows of few more commanding figures, and of none more charming. Springing from a small country, his genius has turned the whole civilized world into a fatherland claiming him for its own. Writing miniature plays for puppet stages, he has taken his place beside Ibsen and Strindberg as a reformer of the modern theatre. Seeking for a form that would fit his dreams even more perfectly than his own "formless" dramas, he has raised the philosophical essay to a height attained only by Emerson among latter-day writers. Though working only for truth and the joy of working, his efforts have also earned worldly returns, enabling him to make a home of an old Benedictine abbey, where Madame Maeterlinck, who on the stage is Georgette Leblanc, can find ideal settings for "Macbeth" and "Pélléas and Mélisande." That such a man should, as rumor asserts, refuse to surrender his Belgian citizenship in order to become a member of the French Academy seems too consistent with his character not to be true.

The charm of this man, who has given us such masterpieces of soul-penetration as "Aglavaine and Selysette" or "Wisdom and Destiny," is rendered doubly striking by a physical ruggedness and balance that furnish a background of unexpectedness to the subtlety of his speculation and the delicacy of his artistic form. Tall and active, large of limb and rather heavy featured, he is more at home out of doors than in the study. Sweeping along the highroads in an automobile driven by himself, or skim-

MAURICE MAETERLINCK 189

ming the frozen surface of some canal in his native country, he appears most himself. Yet there is much both in his appearance and his habits that helps to account for that gentle calm which strikes us as the dominant spirit of his work even when he deals with the heart's most stirring tragedies. Having only the tone of his poetry in mind, Arthur Symons said once that "he speaks always without raising his voice." But that saying holds true of the whole man and all that he is and does.

Seldom has the world known a soul so well poised, so at peace with whatever fate might choose to bring, so disregardful of the petty concerns that keep most human lives in a state of turmoil. All polite conventionalities are hateful to him, and yet he would never dream of striving consciously at any sort of unconventionality. It seems just as natural for him to be himself as this requires effort in ordinary persons. And when thus surrendering to the quiet pressure from within, he cannot but shun the bustle and hustle, the strife and the shamming, of mart and of drawing room.

Next to his unostentatious strength and unfeigned equanimity, the man's most characteristic trait is a shy reserve, behind which lies an almost complete lack of personal vanity, and not, as sometimes happens, a pride so overweening that it dares not expose itself to any rebuff. If caught at the right time and place, he will talk most fascinatingly—about practically anything but himself. But silence is more natural to him than talk, solitude more dear than company. There is in him a craving to dream and to brood that must have got into his very blood out of the mist-laden atmosphere of his native shores. But whenever he does speak —or write—his every expression proves the truth of Alfred Sutro's declaration that, "if the word mystic implies anything of mental fog or obscurity, then Maeterlinck is none."

He springs from Flemish stock that has been settled for something like six centuries

MAURICE MAETERLINCK

in or about Ghent, where he was born in 1862. His childhood was spent in a home where, as in some of his own plays, ships could be seen sailing through what looked to be the back part of the garden. The country and its population of slow, taciturn peasantry seem to have impressed themselves with equal force on the boy. And to this day his work takes much of its dominant coloring from the closely allied tempers of Belgian nature and Belgian people.

Seven years of precious youth were spent in a Jesuit college under a discipline that he himself has described as tyrannical. And yet I cannot recall a single protest in his art evoked by that significant experience. Here as elsewhere he looks kindly to the past and the institutions that once served it well, while all the eagerness of his spirit goes out to the future and what it may bring of higher perfection, higher happiness.

In that college, and later at the university, he met several men of his own kind—men like Charles van Lerberghe and Emile

Verhaeren, whose names hardly mean anything in English-speaking countries, though they have given Belgium a noted place in present-day literature. He studied law and was admitted to the bar. He even practiced a little and lost a case or two. This failure was ascribed to his low and rather thin voice, which lends itself but poorly to emphatic expression. But I suspect that it depended as much on his ability to see both sides of every case. He, who has spoken of our tendency to believe in a universal justice as "the prejudice which has its roots deepest in our hearts," cannot have failed, from the very start, to perceive how the elusive thing we call "right" refuses to stay undivided with any one person or cause.

At twenty-four he went to Paris—to the place where, if we may believe Alfred Sutro, "art is more than a word, more than a cult—a brotherhood." From the first Maeterlinck was received as a member of that brotherhood by the grace of God. The air was then full of a sort of symbolism that endeavored to express by the innate melody of words what might be too elusive for their meaning. And young Maeterlinck wrote poems as hauntingly incomprehensible as any of the rest.

Then he published his first play, "Princess Maleine," and Octave Mirbeau proclaimed him "greater than Shakespeare." Most men would have lost their heads over the ill-worded praise, or their hearts over the ridicule it provoked. Nothing illustrates his wonderful mental equilibrium better than his calm disregard of both applause and laughter. And it was not long before other plays followed—of a quaintness and a daintiness such as the world had never seen before—and with each of them his fame waxed and spread.

What his financial position may have been in those early days I have not been able to discover. But he must have had some private means that enabled him to pursue his course without regard to anything but his own faith in it. And so he has continued to do ever since—"loving what he wrote, and writing only what he loved." Now the day is gone when the authenticity of his genius might be seriously questioned. Probably nothing has done more to settle that question than his fairy play, "The Blue Bird," by which he succeeded in appealing to the many as formerly he had appealed to the few. They tell me that at one time this play was given by fifty-nine different companies in Russia alone. Be that as it may, there is now no civilized language into which his works have not been transplanted. Nor is there a nook so hidden in any part of the Western world that it is not likely to hold some life made a little more livable by his wise musings. And yet one may wonder whether his influence on those more accustomed to lead than to follow is not even more noteworthy, as these words by August Strindberg seem to indicate:

"One can neither steal nor borrow from Maeterlinck. It is even difficult to become his pupil, for there are no free passes that give entrance into his world of beauty. But one may be urged by his example into searching one's own dross-heaps for gold—and it is in this sense that I acknowledge my debt to the master."

To take up his works separately would lead me beyond my present purpose. All I wish to do here is to suggest certain general aspects that seem inseparable from whatever he does—that, in a word, are one with his spirit. Of course, he must be acclaimed a master in the handling of the written word, and his mastery shows itself not the least in the harmony with which his sentences invariably are fraught. But the better part of the beauty springing from his soul lies, nevertheless, in the thoughts to which his words give wings—thoughts like the one shining brightly out of this passage: "Light, though so fragile, is perhaps the one thing of all that yields naught of itself as it faces immensity." Here we have infinity of time and space confined within a few words, spoken "without the air of having said anything more than the simplest observation."

And his work abounds with thoughts that are equally sublime in aspect and in scope. Yet he never lets himself be tempted beyond poetic suggestiveness into scientific exhaustiveness. The sense of things still unuttered always remains the final impression. And perhaps it is in this implied abundance, this limitless reserve power, that his main appeal lies. For it is this side of his nature that has enabled him to look at life and death with such imperturbable eyes. Through that quiescent power, reaching beyond the spoken word into the one not yet breathed, he has carried peace to a time fatigued beyond endurance by an over-long struggle.

For more than one hundred years, up to the closing decade of the last century, the cry was for action, and for ever more action. From Maeterlinck came the first truly inspired call to rest—but not to rest

MAURICE MAETERLINCK

of the Tolstoyan, life-denying kind. The change foreshadowed by his pregnant words was meant to bring man nearer to life's innermost purpose—which he has himself declared to be perfection—and not away from it. For the mark of civilization is, after all, inhibition rather than stimulation. And by constantly accentuating the need for quiet, subconscious preparation, Maeterlinck has done much to dispose of that vaunted strenuousness which too often in the past degenerated into mere meaningless gyration. Not inaction, but action properly determined, is his gospel. If we follow him, then conflict, which is hastened action, will be reduced to a minimum, while combination and cooperation, which stand for action more fully prepared, will take more and more of the world's energy.

Maeterlinck has been called a poet of the subconscious—or I may have called him so myself. The name is good, at any rate, and it finds warrant in the light he has poured into "that holy of holies of the 'Buried

Temple,' in which our most intimate thoughts and the forces that lie beneath them and are unknown to us go in and out without our knowledge and grope in search of the mysterious road that leads to future events." But his main discovery and most significant revelation concerning the subconscious rests in the intimate connection which he has established between certain mysterious powers within ourselves and certain equally mysterious powers on the outside. What he shows—or tries to show—is that these two sets of powers are at bottom identical.

Poetically he has accomplished what Bergson has achieved philosophically. Life, so threatening when lying wholly beyond our own selves, becomes homely and familiar when found at work within those same selves. The fear with which man has regarded fate tends thus to change into happy faith—the unknown becomes the partly known—and in dealing with life, destiny, providence, man begins at last to feel as if

he were but dealing with another self. But
by opening up these new vistas into the
heart of being, where our own image comes
back to us as if mirrored in the pupil of a
loved one's eye, Maeterlinck has done his
share, and a large one at that, toward preparing a religious re-formulation for which
some of the best men on both sides of the
ocean are now working ardently. When
that formulation has been attained, I think
it will be seen that Maeterlinck has contributed not only a conception of life as
trustworthy, but of death as an integral
part of life—and not the unkindliest at that.

Like Tolstoy, like Zola, like so many
other men of strong physique and vivid
imagination, this dreamer from the Low-
lands has been largely preoccupied with the
inevitable moment of dissolution that forms
the interrogation point at the end of every
human career. But while Tolstoy sought
to scare men into righteousness by enhanc-
ing the terror of that ever-present spectre,
one of Maeterlinck's chief tasks has been

to breathe the breath of hope and sympathetic comprehension on our terror, and thus to melt it into vanishing mist. Of course, he began by staring at the spectre in open-eyed horror like the rest of us. For years its grim figure stalked through his plays like a veiled angel of darkness. But gradually there came light into his vision, and that vision widened and grew until all creation lay steeped in brightness. It is that vision he has tried to make ours—in "The Blue Bird," for instance—and when we possess it, then what has hitherto figured in our fancies as life's main curse will undoubtedly change into one of its many blessings.

Looking upon life and death in the way I have just tried to indicate, it is only natural that Maeterlinck should entertain toward humanity a vast tolerance—nay, more than that: an unshakable confidence. At one time a student of Nietzsche, and always a lover of Emerson, he has nevertheless consistently refused to accept any view of the individual as the ultimate object of all existence, or as its supreme arbiter within the scope of human existence. Speaking of universal suffrage, which he holds a necessary step on the road to higher cultural development, he wrote that, "in those problems in which all life's enigmas converge, the crowd which is wrong is almost always justified as against the wise man who is right." Yet he is anything but blind to the part played by the individual as a hand reached out by the race for its own uplifting, and he does not hesitate to assert that, "when the sage's destiny blends with that of men of inferior wisdom, the sage raises them to his level, but himself rarely descends."

The full extent of his foresightedness, as well as the heart of his political faith, is laid bare when he comes to discuss the interaction of those two opposed principles—the racial and the individual. Then he says that, when life below man is concerned, "all genius lies in the species, in life or in nature, whereas the individual is nearly always stupid." But in man, on the other hand—and in man alone—he finds that real emulation exists between the racial and the individual intelligences. In man he finds also a tendency "toward a sort of equilibrium which is the great secret of the future." And in the solving of that secret—the secret of how to make the man with a mission and the mass of ordinary men give each other mutual respect and support—lies the only hope of our modern democracies.

Too often the essential difference between philosophy and wisdom is lost sight of. While all wisdom is based on some philosophical coordination of life's multiplicity, it would be dangerous to find wisdom in all that we now call philosophy. It is not out of place to give the title of philosopher to Maeterlinck—as Professor Dewey has pointed out—but he is more: a sage. Application lurks back of his most abstract speculations, and what he principally wants us to do is to learn in order to live. Both

MAURICE MAETERLINCK 203

the manner and the result of such learning are suggested in this passage: "If we had applied to the removal of various necessities that crush us, such as pain, old age and death, one-half of the energy displayed by any little flower in our gardens, we may well believe that our lot would be very different from what it is."

Somebody has said that he possesses "the child's faculty of wonder." This is true, and one reason for his power over our time is his untiring effort to turn us in childlike wonder toward that ocean of dumb life out of which we have risen into unique articulateness. Like Bergson, he wants to teach us how to soften the noise made by our reasons in order that we may catch the unspoken messages passing from the rest of life into our instincts and intuitions. But to do so, we must cultivate the simplicity of spirit that has lived untainted in his own heart through so many years of conspicuous success—the simplicity that sends him out to watch his beloved bees in the early morn of every day, and that helps him to define the new mysticism he feels coming as "nothing more than a knowledge of self that has far overstepped the ordinary limits of consciousness."

III

Its Philosopher: Henri Bergson

TO make straight for the point of this article: Why should, out of an unobtrusive and unknown French scholar like Professor Henri Bergson, suddenly emerge a figure of world-wide interest and importance?

Ten years ago nobody dwelling outside the inner courts of organized knowledge paid the least attention to his sayings or doings. And to-day the whole civilized world is asking eagerly for the slightest details relating to his private or public life. His books—of which there are only four, not counting his doctor's thesis—have each reached six or seven editions in the original, and they are now being hurriedly translated into one language after another. His teachings are spreading, like flames across a sun-scorched prairie. Everywhere laymen and learned alike feel compelled to define their intellectual, moral and artistic attitudes by reference to his ideas. We find him quoted as their spiritual authority by leaders of the Syndicalist labor movement in France and by the young Tory Democrats of England, by the Modernist reformers within the Catholic Church and by those audacious iconoclasts who, as Post-Impressionists, are startling the world with a new art form.

"He has been accepted by the Symbolists as the philosopher of the new idea," writes an English journalist in regard to the latest movement in French poetry. And the same man informs us that "the intuitional philosophy of Bergson has so taken possession of Paris that the spirit of it seems to fill every place." All this superficial popularity might merely arouse suspicion as to the man's genuine power and scope as a thinker, but when we turn to the other side

—to the world of expert opinion *par preference*—we meet with the same almost unanimous recognition of Bergson's place and influence. "His appearance in the field of philosophy promises to be a turning point in the history of human thought," writes a critic like G. R. T. Ross in the London *Nation,* and from innumerable other quarters the same note of unbounded enthusiasm is heard. Even when his ideas, as such, are bitterly opposed, the learning and ingenuity displayed in their presentation are ungrudgingly acknowledged.

In our search for causes capable of explaining this abrupt rise of a quiet thinker into world-circling fame it is of little use to speak of "faddisms" and "passing fashions." For in the voice of Bergson there is not one sensational note. He has taken no step to attract or hold the attention of the greater public—though he believes passionately in working and writing for nothing less than all men. In his attitude toward truth and its right of way against all selfish interests or established superstitions, he is as uncompromising as any other typical representative of his class. And in spite of his lucid prose, vivid power of illustration, and constant effort at clearness and conciseness, his writings are by no means easy reading to a mind not trained in the ways of systematic thinking. There is, in a word, every reason to assume that his position is founded on true merit, and that, whatever ebb or increasing flood his outward popularity may experience after this, his spirit will become indelibly stamped on the world's thought, so that after having passed through him that thought must for all future be different from what it was before he appeared.

To account for his extraordinary renown to-day, we must assume that his qualities and gifts and achievements are those of men like Descartes and Spinoza, Kant and Hegel, Schopenhauer and Comte, Spencer and James. In each such case, when the efforts of a single man have exercised marked effect not only on all subsequent thinking but on the conduct of the mass of his contemporaries, we have, I think, to lead the result back to three coöperating factors: first, a strong and highly magnetic personality, so that what the man *says* or *does* becomes supported and supplemented by what he *is;* secondly, a distinctly new way of seeing life and interpreting it, whereby man's timidity in front of the world-riddle becomes to some additional degree abated; and thirdly, a particular need on the part of mankind which is administered to by the wider vision of the man in question. We have in this country had a most striking example, in the person of the late William James, of such cooperation between a man's character, his creative thought, and the acute demand of the world at large. And Bergson's case is, I feel sure, another one of the same kind, though perhaps even more remarkable—for did we not hear James himself at the height of his fame apply the title of "master" to the younger and then less known Frenchman?

In his career, as outlined by external facts, there is nothing that will throw much light on his success, though some have traced it in part to his foreign ancestry and cosmopolitan heritage. He is of Jewish and Polish descent, but his family came to France from the other side of the Channel. He himself was born in Paris, but became a Frenchman only by naturalization, obtained after he had already entered the public schools. There must have been a great deal of inherent adaptability in his nature, for neither as student nor as teacher does he ever seem to have been in conflict with his surroundings—a rare fact to mention in the biography of a man of unmistakable genius. Yet he gave early evidence both of ability and originality. At 18 he took a prize in mathematics. And even in his doctor's thesis, finished in 1889, when he was thirty, the ideas which later brought him such renown may be found foreshadowed. When in 1900, after teaching for nearly twenty years in the high schools and normal colleges maintained by the state, he was made professor of modern philosophy in the ancient College of France, at Paris, the eyes of the learned world were already turned expectantly in his direction, and his election to the French Institute a year later came as a matter of course.

It was as a teacher he first began to lay the foundation of his influence on the present generation of Frenchmen, and it is from his success as a teacher that we get valuable light on his progress in general. That his success has been almost phenomenal may be judged by the gloomy forebodings uttered from time to time by leading representatives of older thought currents. Nothing less than a generation of students raised in total scorn of established scientific methods and ideals is what they have professed to fear. Whatever the outcome of it may prove, the fact remains that the great body of students in France is thoroughly inoculated with Bergsonism, while outside of that country the same set of ideas and ideals is conquering one university after another. Thus it is said that the students at Jena are more familiar with the works of the Parisian professor than with the "actualism" expounded by their own venerable preceptor, Rudolf Eucken.

Too often in the past the academic lecturer seems to have measured his accomplishments by the degree of abstruseness he managed to attain. And philosophy has equally often been nothing but an exciting game of hide and seek, with vanity for goad, and for goal alleged "truths" having little or no bearing on the "vulgar" issues of ordinary life. To this entire tendency of what has sometimes been called "mandarinism" the attitude of Bergson has from the start been frankly hostile. He seeks above everything else to make himself clear. And he does so to a large extent by constant reference of his argument to the facts of actual existence. For mere sophistries he has no use whatever. And he takes his place conspicuously with that growing group of thinkers the world over who insist that philosophy, like everything else, must be for all mankind.

What has just been said of his speaking applies with equal truth to his writing. He is a master of style, but one who always insists on making style a servant of the thought to be expressed. An English reviewer says that his written work has "the unity and flow, above all the imagination, of a poem." Nevertheless it is always "loaded" —every line betrays a vast knowledge that is never one-sided or pedantic. Thus the reviewer just quoted wonders at the fact that Bergson shows equal command of "ancient speculation" and of modern biology. Though starting as a mathematician, he has mastered the most difficult art of translating abstract thought into terms of concrete life—as when, to give only one instance, he speaks of consciousness as "a momentary spark flying up from the friction of real actions against possible actions."

So far he has, as already mentioned, produced only four volumes—the first of these in 1889, and the latest one in 1907. The third to be completed and the last to be translated into English was "Le Rire" (Laughter), on which its author spent nearly twenty years of study and thought. It deals with laughter as a social function, the author's leading idea being contained in this sentence: "The function of laughter is to punish and to repress certain actions that appear as defects to the social consciousness." This sharp accentuation of man's social side is very characteristic of Bergson's whole attitude. It colors all his ideas and theories, and in the light of it one finds it hard to understand how some of his avowed but uninvited followers—like the anarchistically inclined Syndicalists—have been able to draw any inspiration from his teachings.

His other three volumes have been brought out here under the following titles: "Time and Free Will," "Matter and Memory," "Creative Evolution." The first two

HENRI BERGSON

deal with certain fundamental problems of consciousness and are more closely specialized than the third. Through them Bergson has endeavored to establish the reality of time—of which he says that "we do not think it, but live it, because life transcends intellect"—and the presence of an element of free choice and consequent unforeseeableness in all of man's actions. In the introduction to "Matter and Memory" occurs a passage that seems to summarize both the basis and the spirit of all that he has written. There are two principles, he says, which he has used as a clue throughout his researches:

"The first is that in psychological analysis we must never forget the utilitarian character of our mental functions, which are essentially turned toward action. The second is that the habits formed in action find their way up to the sphere of speculation, where they create fictitious problems, and that metaphysics must begin by disposing of this artificial obscurity."

From first to last, "Creative Evolution" is largely concerned with the clearing away of just such "artificial obscurities," by which reality has become overlaid in the course of man's millennial groping toward an understanding of it. Beyond all doubt it is Bergson's greatest book, as it is his latest—and the one into which he has put most not only of his system but of himself. The personality of the man—with all its rare treasures of simplicity and sincerity, of insight and of sympathy, of common sense and of fancy—shines gloriously through every one of its pages. And it is in these pages he has given that something which is at once new and fitted to meet the crying need of his time—the something, in other words, that sets him aside as a thinker of creative originality. In this work he has no longer been satisfied to deal with mere isolated phases of life, but has—in accordance with the philosopher's time-honored right—pushed on toward certain universal conclusions, shaping themselves at last into a logical totality of cosmic interpretation.

For the professional philosopher the book is rich in startling and, of course, debatable propositions, with which I shall not concern myself here. For I want to get at the very heart of the Frenchman's thought—the way in which he conceives and meets the riddle of life itself. First of all, then, he finds us using two different instruments in dealing with life, and he draws a sharp distinction between the origin, nature and function, on one side, of instinct, and, on the other, of intellect. The main thing to all philosophy so far has been thought: the main thing to Bergson is the act of living and our unformulated sense of it—that is intuition, or "instinct turned self-conscious."

"Instinct," he says, "is moulded on the very form of life. If the consciousness that slumbers in it could awake, if it were wound up into knowledge instead of being wound off into action, if we could ask and it could answer, it would give up to us the most intimate secrets of life." And he cries to us: "Let us try to see, no longer with the eyes of the intellect alone, which grasps only the already made and which looks from the outside, but with the spirit; I mean with that faculty of seeing which is immanent in the faculty of acting and which springs up, somehow, by the twisting of the will on itself, when action is turned into knowledge, like heat, so to say, into light."

He does not scorn or spurn intellect. On the contrary, its cooperation is needed for the utterance of what is laid bare by intuition. Seen thus, "with the spirit," an essential dualism is found at the bottom of all existence—the dualism between matter and life, between unorganized and organized being. "The vision we have of the material world is that of a weight which falls," he says; "but all our analyses show us, in life, an effort to remount the incline that matter descends." Out of the effort made by life, "the reality which ascends," to overcome, or

HENRI BERGSON

at least to suspend, the downward rush of matter, springs the tangible and visible universe.

Life proper reveals itself above all as a flux and a creation. "To exist is to change, to change is to mature, and to mature is to go on creating oneself endlessly," Bergson tells us. Back of all this creative change he finds a common impetus that he calls the *élan vital*—the life-urge. We may imagine it as "a centre from which worlds shoot out like rockets in a fire-works display." As here, so it is at work everywhere, shaping, developing, initiating. "It is probable that life goes on in other planets, in other solar systems also, under forms of which we have no idea." For life, in the eyes of Bergson, is neither an accident nor a voluntary act of some supernatural being: it is a universal necessity.

Evolution he sees not as a straight line, but as a sheaflike divergence of forms. Some lines come quickly to an end. Others stretch onward with constant offshoot of new branches. Each onward step has to be bought by the surrender of something that until then had remained common property, and which thereafter will become characteristic of a parallel form. Thus, for instance, the vegetable kingdom represents chiefly the general tendency of life to store up energy, while the animal kingdom specializes, so to speak, in the expenditure of energy.

To Bergson each form appears as a narrowly restricted delegate of the life-urge, devised for a distinct purpose, and permitted to regard this purpose as the end of all life. "Each species, each individual even, retains only a certain impetus from the universal vital impulsion, and tends to use this energy in its own interest." Hence the egoism that marks each separate species as well as specimen. The principal social significance of Bergson's ideas, however, lies in his statement that "everywhere the tendency to individualize is opposed and at the same time completed by an antagonistic and complementary tendency to associate." The evolu-

HENRI BERGSON

tion of being in this double direction is due to the very nature of life. Thus "society, as soon as formed, tends to melt the associated individuals into a new organism, so as to become itself an individual, able in its turn to be part and parcel of a new association." Beyond the human mind we divine the race-mind: behind the individual will, an all-inclusive world-will.

When we have reached this point we have also reached the most comprehensive aspect of Bergson's thought—an aspect which Professor Lovejoy has indicated by his reference, in the works of more than one prominent thinker of to-day, to "a genuinely radical evolutionism, which is at the same time of a highly romantic and religious spirit." It is nothing less than a new religious formulation that seems to shape itself before our rapt vision when Bergson says that God, as defined in the light of the life-urge theory, "has nothing of the already made," but is "unceasing life, action, freedom." Another vista of equally startling nature is opened up by his assertion that "the whole of humanity, in space and in time, is one immense army galloping beside and before and behind each of us in an overwhelming charge, able to beat down every resistance and clear the most formidable obstacles, perhaps even death."

A divine principle, lying ahead and not behind us; an immortality not miraculously conferred but logically attained: these appear to be some of the possibilities contained in Bergson's audacious conclusions. And it is undoubtedly through his courage in drawing out the consequences of his own thoughts thus far—and through his ability to do so without for a moment losing his firm hold on the actuality with which we are all familiar—that he has won his dominant place not only in the heads of the few but in the hearts of the many.

Like President Eliot, like the late Professor James, like all those earnest and able men who are banded together in the world-embracing Monistic Union, Bergson must feel that much of what still passes current as religion has lost its background of actual experience, while at the same time the need of man to relate himself to the unknown as well as to the known has grown no less poignant than it was in the past. And to him more than to anybody else, as I see it, has it been given to restate the truths of being in such manner that they become, not a religion in themselves, but the firm basis on which a new and more reverential conception of the great insolvable mysteries of life may be reared.

GRAAL KNIGHTS OF MODERN LETTERS

I

GEORGE GISSING

"THE name of Henry Ryecroft never became familiar to what is called the reading public. A year ago obituary paragraphs in the literary papers gave such account of him as was thought needful: the date and place of his birth, the names of certain books he had written, an allusion to his work in the periodicals, the manner of his death. At the time it sufficed. Even those few who knew the man, and in a measure understood him, must have felt that his name called for no further celebration."

These opening words of the preface to "The Private Papers of Henry Ryecroft," the last book by Gissing published during

GEORGE GISSING

his lifetime, were prophetic of what happened when the man who wrote them actually died in 1904, carried away less by disease than by his own inability to husband his vital resources. A leading New York daily, which prides itself on being rather more "literary" than its rivals, disposed of the event in three lines. Most of the other newspapers said nothing at all. To the public at large the news carried no significance whatever.

Gissing was never popular. He knew it and accepted the fact without resentment. Public favor was not his object. At the very beginning of his career as writer, he set up for himself an artistic ideal and pronounced an artistic creed to which he remained faithful to the end. Neither ideal nor creed was of a kind tending to make him one of the public's pampered, much-advertised and much-selling favorites. Both are found in "The Unclassed."

This was not his first book, appearing four years later than the almost forgotten

"Workers in the Dawn." But it was the first one in which the true temper of Gissing's art found adequate expression. Like "The Private Papers," it is largely, if not wholly, autobiographical. The central figure, *Osmond Waymark,* is Gissing himself. *Waymark,* who gave up teaching to pursue the literary vocation, just as his creator had done, says:

"Let me get a little more experience, and I will write a book such as no one has yet ventured to write, at all events in England. Not *virginibus puerisque* will be my book, I assure you, but for men and women who like to look beneath the surface, and who understand that only as artistic material has human life any significance."

Gissing wrote not only one book, but many of the kind he promised in that first mature work of his, which appeared in 1884. He wrote "The Nether World," "New Grub Street," "In the Year of Jubilee," "The Whirlpool," "Our Friend the Charlatan," and nearly a score more of novels and short stories. The works just named are those which, in my opinion, reach the high-water mark of his achievement. This means that they must be counted among the strongest pieces of imaginative writing contained in modern Anglo-American literature. But all his works, even those in which his genius seemed to flag and lose itself under the harassments of an adverse fate, display, although in less degree, the traits that place him so far beyond and above the common herd of caterers to the literary taste of the public. Sincerity of purpose, shrewdness of observation, depth of sympathy, and command of form are some of the qualities common to them all.

If they fail, it is in not being entertaining in the accepted sense of the day. Each of them is a piece of life, terrible at times in its reality, but never loathsome. They are the creations of a man who had the courage to face life as he found it, and who vowed to describe it as he saw it, not as his readers might like it to appear. Of revolting naturalism in details there is next to none. Even when dealing with the life led by the lowest and most unfortunate of human beings, the women of the streets, Gissing showed a reserve in the handling of his material, without ever missing the desired effect, which might be offered as an object lesson to many European writers and some in this country. No, what scares away the reader who comes to his pages in search of amusement only is the note of sadness that sounds through most of them, the assertion again and again of the spirit which once prompted Gissing to declare that: "Art, nowadays, must be the mouthpiece of misery, for misery is the keynote of modern life."

Those words might have been written by Strindberg. In fact, there is much in Gissing that reminds the reader of the Swede, and their pessimistic outlook on life was essentially identical, just as the causes producing their viewpoints had much resemblance. Gissing, however, proved himself much more capable of separating his own fate from the general course of life, without confusion of the two. He was braver as a man, less given to make his art the vehicle of personal grievances, though in power and skill and dynamic penetration he fell far short of the man who wrote "The Dance of Death" and "Inferno."

A man writing words like those quoted above, and meaning them, could of course never be popular, hardly even with the critics. What better warrant could there be for the charge brought by a newspaper at the time of his death—that of his "taking a gloomy view of life." Yet I might quote "The Town Traveller" and "The Crown of Life" as evidence against the truth of that charge, but it may be better, after all, to let it stand. If Gissing's view of life was sombre and sober, there was, as I have already hinted at, so much in his own existence to account for it. Of his life, as of Strindberg's, misery was the keynote, indeed.

While a mere lad he had to begin earning

his own livelihood. After a period of relatively carefree but utterly uncongenial toiling, the day came at last when the voice within could no longer be silenced. Literature was to be his calling. The start was made under conditions that might have deterred the most temerarious, and for years his steps were dogged by hunger and many shaped hardships. He lived in cellars. He ate his meals in places that would have offered a way-wearied tramp chances for criticism. His breakfast consisted often of a slice of bread and a drink of water—and too often it was the one meal of the day. Four-and-sixpence a week paid for his lodging. A meal that cost more than a sixpence was a feast. The ordinary comforts of modern life were unattainable luxuries to him. Once when a newly posted notice in the lavatory of the British Museum warned readers that "the basins were to be used for casual ablutions only," he was abashed and startled because of his own complete dependency on the facilities of the place.

Through all the hard years he remained alone, foregathering with none of the Bohemian clusters that abound in London, and having only one friend to converse with.

And through all that misery and squalor and soul-breaking poverty he pursued the aim he had set for himself with indomitable, never-flinching persistency and courage, quaking at heart now and then, but never imagining himself for a moment a hero or a martyr.

"I had a goal before me, and *not* the goal of the average man," he exulted years later in an hour of retrospection. "Even when pinched with hunger, I did not abandon my purposes, which were of the mind." And again this of his mental attitude at the time: "How surprised and indignant I should have felt had I known of any one who pitied me."

Homer and Shakespeare were his constant companions in those days, lying within easy reach on the corner of "the filthy deal table" that served as his writing desk. To find money for the purchase of books, which to him were a necessity as much as the air he breathed, he had often to forego a meal. For six years he trod the pavements of London "without stepping once on mother earth" or being able to satisfy his passionate love and longing for nature. At times he suffered from prolonged, savage headaches. Medical treatment was out of the question. All he could do was to lock his door, go to bed, and lie there, without food or drink, till he became able to look after himself again.

There can be slight doubt that those years laid the foundation of a structural weakness which rendered resistance impossible when the critical moment arrived. Those were the days of violent radicalism, when he lectured to workingmen's clubs, "knew what it was to feel the heart burn with wrath and envy of the privileged classes," and fought for the freedom of the poor and the ignorant "because he was himself in the bondage of unsatisfiable longing." Echoes of them are found in "Demos" and "The Nether World."

Then came better days, with "assurance of food and clothing for half a year at the time." He had, to use his own words again, succeeded in pleasing and making himself a profit to the editors and publishers who represented the vague throng of readers—his actual employers. He was able at last to satisfy his fondness for nature and for travelling.

The autobiographical character of "The Unclassed" has been mentioned. It is chiefly the story of a young woman whose love for *Osmond Waymark* gives her strength to reclaim herself from the life of shame into which fate rather than her own fault had forced her. In the end she is married to him, and the happiness of their union seems assured. Gissing married twice—first a woman of the kind just indicated, and later a servant girl. Both marriages were unhappy, and out of them grew the worst clouds that overshadowed the middle years of his life, retarding his growth, cramping his powers and embittering his mind still further. But he fought and conquered sorrow as previously he had gained victory in his battle with poverty and distress. Of the appearance and mental and moral make-up of the man who finally emerged from that double test, I like to think in the terms employed by Gissing himself for the picturing of *Osmond Waymark:*

"There was nothing commonplace in his appearance and manner; one divined in him a past out of the ordinary range of experiences, and felt the promise of a future which would, in one way or another, be remarkable. . . . There was a ring in his voice which inspired faith; whatever might be his own doubts and difficulties—and his face testified to his knowledge of both—it was so certain that he had power to overcome them."

Add to this the description of *Henry Ryecroft* in the preface to "The Private Papers": "He had suffered much from defeated ambition, from disillusions of many kinds, from subjection to grim necessity; the result of it was not a broken spirit, but a mind and temper so sternly disciplined, that, in ordinary intercourse with him, one did not know but that he led a calm, contented life."

Just such I like to imagine the man who, to my thinking, broke important new paths for the English novel, besides treading the old ones with so much success. Many have already followed where he led the way. As early as 1884 he wrote: "The fact is, the novel of everyday life is getting worn out. We must dig deeper, to yet untouched social strata."

He did what he preached. That was years before the name of Gorky was ever heard of. Having explored the nethermost depths, Gissing ascended a few steps and began to devote his attention to a social stratum of which he speaks in "Our Friend the Charlatan" as: "That vague multitude between the refined middle class and the rude toilers, which plays such an important part in modern civilization. Among these people, energy is naked, motives are direct. There the strength and the desires of the people become vocal."

The results of this new venture were "In the Year of Jubilee" and "The Town Traveller," two of his most remarkable books, in which we are introduced to a class of people that have never before appeared in literature, as it seems to me. Such figures as the three sisters in the former book and the town traveller himself, the sprightly, irrepressible, wide-hearted *Mr. Gammon,* have about them a freshness and an originality which lend additional bitterness to the thought that the pen of their creator had to be laid down so prematurely.

Gissing's drawing of character was never permitted to become caricature. Whether dealing with some titled aristocrat or some grotesque shape from the slums, half man, half beast, he went about his task with the same unprejudiced regard for truth, and for truth only. But the final explanation of his success lies in the sympathy which he gave to all his figures. "The artist should be free from everything like moral prepossession," he wrote once.

This principle may be seen at work throughout his books. There is no judging or sorting of good and bad. Each character is allowed to stand on its merits. The author states facts, but does not condemn. *Harvey Rolfe* in "The Whirlpool"—one of the most attractive figures drawn by Gissing and one of the finest specimens of true manhood that ever captured a reader's heart and fancy—is not treated with more consideration or forbearance than the wretched *Harriet Castle* in "The Unclassed" or "Our Friend the Charlatan," the slick *Mr. Dyce Lashmar*.

Love and art were regarded by this alleged pessimist as the moving principles of life, and only by their pursuit could life get meaning. "Beauty is the solace of life, and love is the end of being," he said in one place. Humor of the conventional kind he never essayed. Yet he was not incapable of comprehending and appreciating the humor that springs spontaneously out of life, as may be seen in "The Unclassed" when *O'Gree* and his *Sally* meet and make love in the mummy room of the British Museum for want of a more appropriate trysting-place.

The day will come, I think, and soon enough, when Gissing will be read and treasured according to his desert. In the meantime the admirers of his art—a growing host—will have to bear in mind the manly words he used in "The Private Papers" in reference to himself: "The world has done me no injustice. Why should any man who writes, even if he write things immortal, nurse anger at the world's neglect? For the work of man's mind there is one test, and one alone, the judgment of generations yet unborn. If you have written a great book, the world to come will know of it."

he debated long and earnestly with himself which language to choose for his medium: French or English. The story has the virtue of not being inherently impossible. But I doubt nevertheless its authenticity, for at fifteen he had made up his mind not only to become a sailor, but a British sailor; and when, at nineteen, in the harbor of Marseilles, he heard a few words of English spoken for the first time out of an English mouth, that event impressed itself so strongly on his mind that, a score of years later, he was moved to make it the closing event of the reminiscent volume he has named "A Personal Record."

As a boy of eight he read his first Shakespeare play, "Two Gentlemen of Verona," in a Polish translation made by his father. At ten he had read most of Victor Hugo's works. A little later he became acquainted with the novels of Dickens, and devoured them eagerly—in Polish. To this day Dickens is one of his firm favorites, another one being Henry James. As a student at the university of Cracow, or travelling with a tutor who himself was a man of unusual promise, he must have gathered up a store of conventional learning. Yet he has said of himself that "the studies came hard to him," and the tutor had to give up the attempt of driving the sea out of his mind. When, at nineteen, he forced his despairing relatives into letting him follow his natural bent, his action represented, to use his own happy phrase, "a standing jump out of his racial surroundings and conditions."

His first experiences as a sailor were obtained in small vessels on the Mediterranean, and on a West Indian trip in a French ship that had to be pumped all the way to keep it from sinking. But very soon he made his way to England, the land of his dreams, finding his first employment in a coasting vessel. The Far East, another cherished goal, he did not reach until he had won a mate's certificate. From an eastern city, Bangkok, he started out with his first command, which made him master of a 500-

ton bark. During his twenty years at sea, he tasted all the hardships, all the vicissitudes, and all the adventures, bad and good, that used to form an inevitable part of a sailor's lot. As a seaman, whether stationed before the mast or on the quarter-deck, he *made good*. There, as later, the indispensable qualities of the artist told. And though, with a touch of melancholy seldom found in him, he has told us that all the long and trying years at sea brought him nothing but "a dozen or so of commendatory letters," we, who have read his books, know that those years brought him something more: a sense of life's fullness and seriousness that has proved the steadying principle of his art, keeping it forever from entering the shallow waters where, side by side, wait cheap success and sure oblivion.

What moved Conrad to try his hand at writing was, according to himself, "a hidden, obscure necessity, a completely masked and unaccountable phenomenon," and not "the famous need of self-expression which artists find in their search for motives." Previously he had written nothing but letters, and few of those. He had never "made a note of a fact, of an impression or of an anecdote," and "the conception of a planned book was entirely outside his mental range when he sat down to write"—in furnished rooms at Pimlico Square, London.

The truth of it seems to be that the germ of a story, a striking figure calling for artistic re-embodiment, had chanced across his path while the first glow of the East was still fresh in his mind. For years he carried it about with him as a haunting possibility. And at last resistance became impossible. Thus "Almayer's Folly" came into being, but not in one stroke. Five years lay between the writing of the first and the last chapters of that book, which, when published in 1895, brought him a great deal of immediate recognition.

During those five years Conrad travelled back and forth over the face of the earth.

JOSEPH CONRAD

Some chapters were written in those rooms at Pimlico Square; others in the equatorial regions of Africa, on board a steamer frozen fast in the Seine at Rouen, in a hydropathic establishment near Geneva, and in a waterside warehouse at London. Twice the manuscript was nearly lost: once in the Congo rapids, and another time in a hotel at Warsaw. During a journey to Australia, the author submitted nine finished chapters to one of the passengers, a Cambridge graduate, with the question: "Is it worth finishing?" All the answer he got was: "Decidedly!"

There are now, as I have already said, sixteen volumes to his credit—nine novels of varying length, five collections of short stories, a volume of reminiscent essays dealing with the sea, and another volume of frankly personal character. Between them, those works cover the five continents. But most of the stories deal with life on the high seas and in the tropics. I believe that no other writer has surpassed Conrad in the

NOTE.—Morley Roberts's "The Private Life of Henry Maitland" fell into my hands while I was preparing this volume for the press. It enabled me to correct a few mistaken dates and facts, but it caused no desire to change the spirit of what I wrote just after Gissing's death.

II

Joseph Conrad

IF some one asked me suddenly to define the fundamental nature of art, I should answer unhesitatingly: it is interpretative imitation of life. This universal characteristic of all true art indicates also where lies Joseph Conrad's claim to world-wide renown. He is one who copies life in such manner that, to the beholder, it becomes more intelligible, and thereby more livable. But even as an artist he holds a place apart, appearing to us a sort of modern knight of the Holy Graal, seeking ever the wondrous vessel in which beauty, worth and truth are said to mingle in triune radiance.

Imitation of life in artistic form demands

JOSEPH CONRAD

above all else on discipline—a simple-hearted subordination of one's own self to something that lies beyond it. And this subordination must neither be timid nor cringing, as truth cannot come out of fear or flattery. The form that we call artistic stands for interpretation, whereby the rhythmic pulse of life is rendered sensible to us. And for such interpretation is needed an insight almost divine in its penetration. Finally, for the blending of discipline and insight into a single-minded acceptance of whatever life may present, without effort at a final judgment that could be given only by omniscience, the artist needs endless sympathy with every aspect and utterance of that vital flow of which all visible and audible things are but so many shadows and echoes.

Discipline, sympathy, insight are the indispensable qualities of an inspired artist. And these are the qualities that have shaped Conrad's strange career, turning an inland lad into a deep-sea sailor, and making a master of English out of one who "did not know six words of the language" when he was nineteen. Up to the end of 1912, he had to his credit sixteen volumes of fiction and reminiscences, not counting his one play or the two novels produced in collaboration with another man. In 1908 no less a critic than John Galsworthy remarked of his first ten volumes that they probably constituted "the only writing of the last twelve years that would enrich the English language to any great extent." And more recently Conrad has had the none too common honor of being granted a small pension out of the British civil list. Considering the obstacles he has had to overcome in order to gain such recognition, one may well be tempted into describing his achievement as unique.

He was born in 1857, somewhere in Poland. His full name was Joseph Conrad Korzeniowski, and that name he retained until his first book appeared in print. His family belonged to the landed gentry of Poland, but as a mere child, while sharing the exile of his parents, he had to learn the hard lessons of poverty and privation. His father was a student, a writer, and a dreamer: one who translated Shakespeare and Hugo into Polish and tried to use his pen for the preservation of the threatened Polish nationality. His mother risked unflinchingly her own life in order to share her husband's exile.

The shadow of Russian despotism fell blightingly on the child's most sensitive years. It killed his mother outright by forcing her to take a long journey when already seriously ill. Her death hastened that of her husband. In his maternal uncle's home, where the orphaned boy found a refuge, there was hardly a face that did not speak of sorrow and suffering earned by the heroic support of a lost cause. Under the spur of those early impressions, the boy dreamt of joining the Turks in their war against Russia. And it is indeed a wonder that the man who grew out of that boy did not put a still worse sting into the irony that saturates, and even a little mars, so many pages in his recent Russian novel, "Under Western Eyes."

While still a boy, his mind was mightily drawn by everything connected with travelling and exploration. At the age of ten, he put his finger on the large blank space which then formed the heart of Africa on all maps and said: "When I grow up, I will go there." And so he did more than twenty years later. Among the belongings he carried with him and nearly lost on that trip up the Congo river to Stanley Falls was the manuscript of the first few chapters of "Almayer's Folly," his first book. And out of the same trip came by and by that marvellous story of his, "Heart of Darkness," which, in its own way, is probably without a peer in all literature.

He was never aware of learning to read—so early in his life did that momentous event take place. But at six he learned French from a governess. There is a story to the effect that, when at last he took to writing, picturing of those two fields of human endeavor—the endlessly variable sea, and the tropics, where life and death, fierce passion and dreamy languor, are always found close together, like twin kernels within a single shell. And so vivid are his pictures, so keen is his analysis, that he makes us positively *sense* the regions described by him. In other words, he enables us to experience vicariously, whether it be the tropics or the ocean, with almost the same acuteness and accuracy as if our experiences were being obtained at first hand. And this is undoubtedly the first and foremost mission of the poet.

To achieve that effect, Conrad has first of all his power of evoking vivid images, as when he tells us how "the ship became a high and lonely pyramid gliding, all shining and white, through the sunlit mist." With this picturesqueness in the best sense goes an equally notable power of characterization, of making us grasp situations or souls by means of some felicitous phrase that cannot be forgotten. Thus he says of *Captain Mitchell* in "Nostromo" that "he was too pompously and innocently aware of his own existence to observe that of others."

Back of each happy expression lies his merciless faculty of observation. He sees everything, and sees it right. When *Singleton,* the Nestor in the forecastle of the Narcissus, turned the pages of the book he was reading, "the muscles of his big white arms rolled slightly under the smooth skin." Little touches of reality, so subtle that not one man in a thousand would think of them, and yet so palpably true that without them the story would seem incomplete, meet us constantly. Here is an instance. When, in "The Nigger of the Narcissus," the disgusted crew inspected the forecastle which had been flooded by the storm, they found the ship's cat miraculously saved. Then some one brought a bucket of fresh water, and "Tom, lean and mewing, came up with every hair astir and had the first drink." But Conrad's realism is never satisfied with mere surface appearances. The souls of things and of men shine through his words and carry us on to a new understanding.

As he can take us to any part of the globe and make us at home there, so he knows every mood of man and how to make us share it. Tragedy and farce find him equally ready and equally impartial. For sheer pathos some of his passages have rarely been excelled—as the one that tells of the final revelation of *Razumov's* guilt to *Nathalie Haldin* in "Under Western Eyes." And when there is a laugh to be had out of the life he is dealing with, he can be gently ironical, as when he lets *Captain McWhirr* in "Typhoon" read up "the chapter on the winds" while the storm is breaking; or he can give us screaming farce as in "Almayer's Folly," when *Babalatchi,* "the statesman of Sambir," has to spend his night grinding out "Trovatore" on a hand organ to sooth the disturbed soul of his master.

Conrad's art, of course, is no more flawless than anything else of human origin. Fault has been found with his apparent disregard of chronological order. But what seems like careless rambling is intentional, and though at times carried a little too far, it adds to the verisimilitude of his stories by giving them an air of genuine reminiscences. More serious is his disregard of the modern demand that the course of events involved in the tale shall be seen through the eyes of a single personality, and that nothing shall be told but what could naturally be known to that one observer. Of this mistake, however, Conrad is not guilty in his later works, although in some of these, like "Nostromo," he has frankly assumed the position and knowledge of an omniscient creator, to whom not only the actions but even the thoughts of every actor in the drama lie wholly open. This marks a return to artistic conventions now generally discarded and condemned, and only his success in making the reader forget everything but the tale itself can be quoted in his defense.

Galsworthy has said that in Conrad's novels "nature is first, and man second." That is not true. In every one of his stories man might be said to constitute "the main show." Nature is present in abundance, but only as seen and heard and felt by man. Conrad himself has declared that "it is we alone who, swayed by the audacity of our minds and the tremors of our hearts, are the sole artisans of all the wonder and romance of the world." A typical instance of man's central position in his work may be found in the part played by the snow-capped dome of Higuerota in "Nostromo": ever-present, dominating the entire landscape, but perceived by us only through the eyes of old *Viola* gazing from the doorway of his inn at the eternal snows.

But while the adventures of men, physical and spiritual, give Conrad his themes, and while he might be expected to remain satisfied if only those men seem sufficiently convincing in their uncompromising individualities, there is in his works something more, something still bigger, something of which he may or may not be conscious himself. Through all of them runs a strange but unmistakable symbolism. Each novel and story seems to stage some elementary passion in many shades and variations.

The storm has been called the hero of "Typhoon." It is no more so than the Chinese fighting for silver dollars in the 'tween-deck. The storm, the boat, the crew, the rest of the officers, are little more than so much background for the figure of *Captain McWhirr*. And while *McWhirr* is as real to us as words can make him, he, in his turn, is but a symbol for a human quality— that of courage. And what we learn from him is that courage has very little to do with the brain, and very much with such simpler functions as circulation and digestion. And if, in this light, we re-examine the other figures standing out in low relief behind that of the captain, we find every one embodying some different form of courage, or lack of it.

In "The Nigger of the Narcissus" the real hero is not *Jimmy,* the colored giant who deceives the others only to die self-deceived, but the crew as a whole. As a crew it is divided within itself, not by man standing against man, but by the conflict of two antagonistic emotions within the breast of every man. The emotions in question are those of pity and cruelty—both thriving side by side in primitive man, but so that one of them marks the past out of which he is emerging, while the other one points toward the future that is his goal.

In "Nostromo" the dominant quality, recurring in every character except that of *Mrs. Gould,* is vanity. But to recognize this fact we must understand that vanity and ambition, pride and aspiration, represent distinctions only of degree. Here as elsewhere what we call virtue began under forms that now look appallingly vicious. From the crude, childish greed for public

JOSEPH CONRAD 257

acclaim found in the glorious *capataz de cargadores* to that "ideal conception of his disgrace" which *Dr. Monygham* had made for himself, or from the intellectual scepticism of a *Decoud* to the mystical materialism of a *Holroyd,* may seem a far cry, indeed—but even such distances can be bridged by evolution, just as they have been bridged by Conrad's inimitable art.

A man who has looked so deeply and so shrewdly into the human heart might be expected to confess some social purpose. This Conrad will not do. He is the artist, the observer—not the judge or the reformer. Saints and knaves find equal justice at his hands, his one avowed object being to reveal man to himself. All political creeds look pretty much alike to him. Remedies for evil there may be—must be—but not in programmes. Not even the sacred name of freedom can cast a spell over him. If there be any principle that to him appears hallowed, it is that of discipline—not the discipline exerted by one man over another, but that which makes each man a master of himself. When this kind of discipline becomes universal, and particularly when it joins hands with sympathy and insight, with love and knowledge, then freedom will result automatically. In this faith of Conrad's—if he is willing to admit it as such—must be sought the most plausible reason for his failure to grasp and convincingly present a single human type: the anarchistic enthusiast for liberty in the abstract.

For religious and philosophical formulations he has little more use than for political programmes. But his pages overflow with true wisdom, with revelations that teach us how to live, not theoretically but practically—as when he tells us that "both men and ships want to have their merits understood rather than their faults found out." Even a man like Maeterlinck has little more to give in this respect—and with the Belgian dreamer's outlook on life Conrad has much in common. The bearing and basis of his own outlook of this kind Conrad has made plain beyond his wont in "A Personal Record," where the following passage suggests at once an artistic and a philosophical creed:

"The ethical view of the universe involves us in the last instance in so many cruel and absurd contradictions, amongst which the last vestiges of pity, hope, charity, and even of reason itself, seem ready to perish, that I have come to suspect that the aim of creation cannot be ethical at all. I would fondly believe that its object is purely spectacular: a spectacle for awe, love, adoration, or hate, if you like, but in this view, and in this view alone, never for despair. Those visions, delicious or poignant, are a moral end in themselves. The rest is our affair—the laughter, the tears, the tenderness, the indignation, the high tranquility of a steeled heart, the detached curiosity of a subtle mind—that's our affair."

TWO STUDIES OF ROBERT HERRICK

I

THERE are writers with numerous volumes to their credit whose art may easily be summarized in a few lines. Robert Herrick is not one of them. And yet he cannot be called versatile in the accepted sense. From first to last, his production seems to have followed certain clearly defined lines, in form and thought and spirit. Though now and then venturing into the realm of verse, he is above all a writer of prose. And though from time to time he has put out charming short stories, his true field is undoubtedly the novel. Moreover, in this field most particularly his own, he adheres closely to a manner of narration that had reached perfection even in his earliest books. Nor is it of any use to search his works for sudden changes of opinion, or for moods contrasting sharply against the prevailing temperamental background. For nearly fifteen years he appears, on the whole, to have been moved by the same spirit, the same outlook on life, the same conception of its deeper realities, the same intense craving to place the truth uppermost. Not as if I meant to say that he has not changed and grown, but his growth has moved him onward along lines distinctly foreshadowed from the first moment he endeavored to gain the ear of the public.

If it be found difficult, as I have found it, to characterize him in a few quick sentences, the cause of it must be sought mainly in the width of his horizons. To define him is, in a way, to define the American people itself. For among writers of recent times, living or dead, there is hardly any one who, in my opinion, has come nearer deserving the epithet "national." In saying this, I am not having in mind the relatively subordinate fact that Herrick moves his scene from one end of the country to another, giving us in the same volume faithful pictures of New England and the West, of the big city and the man-starved country. He is national for no less reason than the full, free reflection of our vast American panorama on every page, in every sentence, of all his larger works. Like a true artist, he is always working in terms of individual life, placing before us a gallery of real men and women such as very few American writers can be credited with; but in what happens to these individuals we find mirrored what is at the same time happening to the nation in its entirety. Strikes, panics, country-wide unrests, "booms" reaching from ocean to ocean, political and ethical fluctuations—these are present not only as painted backgrounds, hanging flatly and stiffly behind the moving creatures in the foreground, but as vital factors, affecting intimately the daily lives of the simplest and humblest.

This being so, one might expect to find Herrick widely read and highly praised. But only one of his books, "Together," can be said to have met with a truly popular success. And among the critics he has gained his just dues only from a few discerning spirits. Again I venture an explanation that has occurred to me. All of Herrick's novels show plenty of "action," even when that word is applied in the narrower sense which makes it almost synonymous with violence. His men and women live and love, fight and strive, suffer and rejoice. The problems and the motives that move them are strong and real. The sex note, so long dominant in all poetry that it has become indispensable, may be heard from one cover to another in his books. Business, nowadays the "theme" to which writers in the fashion turn with increasing absorption, is treated by him with unusual insight and insistency. But for all this the real happenings of each story lie within the dim confines of human souls. His novels are at bottom psychological: physical movements have value in them only in so far as they render visible the subtle movements of the spirit within. And I fear that our general reading public still lacks the intellectual passion that alone can end its timidity in the face of this deeper aspect of life.

This man who deals so audaciously and so cunningly with the secret forces that push and hem not only our private but our public existencies is still young. Born in 1868 at Cambridge, Mass., Herrick has spent almost all his life in the shadow of some great educational institution. A graduate of Harvard, he taught first in his own university and then at the University of Chicago, where he has been professor of English since 1893. Now and then it has been hinted that his art may have taken the better and larger share of his time and energy. But if my information be correct, he has the deepest respect and affection for his original profession, and he goes on teaching from year to year not merely to draw a salary, but because he is devoted to the teacher's mission and has faith in his own ability to fill it. And I am told that he has from the first exerted a marked influence over the students with whom he has come in contact.

Having always held that the author's private life tends rather to obscure than to illumine his art, Herrick has kept his own personality so scrupulously in the background that hardly an item of the usual silly gossip has found its way into print. What little has become known of his private existence seems to show him capable of rising above his own idiosyncrasies to full and clear understanding of currents with which he has no inherent sympathy. He knows and loves every form of art, and some of the stories told about him indicate an almost uncanny sensitiveness to formal perfection. Yet every one of his books may be regarded as a plea for an "ethical" rather than "esthetical" conception both of life and art.

Beginning with "The Gospel of Freedom," which appeared in 1898, every one of his novels would richly deserve a detailed analysis such as cannot come in question here. I have already referred to the dominant note of "nationalism" as opposed to our all too frequent and futile "localism," that runs through them all. Another note, no less prevalent, may be described as social, and as such it may properly be placed in opposition to that overweening demand for individual expression which was characteristic of so much literature belonging to the past century. This is the more surprising as Herrick himself seems at heart to be strongly individualistic both in his sympathies and his proclivities. Nothing but true insight can account for this conquest of innate tendencies—an insight that finds one of its most striking formulations in a sentence from "The Web of Life," where he says that: "In striving restlessly to get plunder and power and joy, men weave the mysterious web of life for ends no human mind can know."

There is in this sentence also a distinct touch of mysticism that stands in sharp contrast to the realistic means generally employed by Herrick. And as we go on from novel to novel, we find this element more and more tangible, though never permitted to intrude itself to an extent that might obscure the everyday clearness of events and characters. Even Van Harrington, the man who began his career in the prisoner's pen of a Chicago police court, and whom we are permitted to follow to the doors of the United States Senate, has this to say of his own experience: "All my life has been given to practical facts, yet I know that at the end of all things there are no facts." In "A Life for a Life" this suggestion of vague, deep-lying realities, too subtle for clear formulation, swells into orchestral power, so that the whole work is colored by it and becomes intelligible only in so far as our own souls are open to its appeal.

With this novel Herrick advanced beyond his naturalistic starting-point. There he occupied ground which had been previously cleared by men like Ibsen, Tolstoy and Maeterlinck. It is an immense allegory, but not of the kind that Bunyan gave us. Rather there is a kinship with that Greek sculpture which distilled the all-human out of the fleeting humanity of the moment. Yet this art, which makes so strongly for the typical, is impressionistic at the same time, abandoning no whit of what the nineteenth century gained along these lines, and insisting sharply on the uniqueness of the individual moment. And it is in this tendency to combine apparently opposed and incompatible qualities that I seek the determining characteristic of the poetry still to come.

II

MY first brief estimate of Herrick's art was written in 1910, just after he had published "A Life for a Life." Since then he has given us only one more volume, "The Healer," which appeared late in 1911. It would not be enough to say that this novel disappointed me: it forced me to revise my conception of its author's position in American letters. In the past I was strongly inclined to think him the Moses destined to lead our literature out of its long desert wandering into the promised land of mature achievement and self-realization. Such a hope I dare hardly hold now. Herrick is still to me one of the foremost writers of fiction we have in this country—if not the foremost. He is one of the few on this side of the ocean who, in rank, approach men like Wells and Conrad and Galsworthy on the other. I feel no desire to withdraw what I have said in praise of his work up to a certain point. But I have come to fear that the point in question may mark the crest of his possible achievement. For years to come he will undoubtedly go on writing big, fine books, as he has done in the past, and we shall continue grateful for each new one. His delicate craftsmanship and genuine psychological insight will as surely assert themselves in the future with no less power than in the past. Yet all this—and it implies a very great deal—cannot make up for a certain lack of faith without which further growth seems to me very doubtful.

I find it hard to indicate the character of this faith with any degree of exactness. It is partly philosophical and partly religious, yet not identical with any philosophical system or religious creed. It looks toward life in its entirety without necessarily calling for any systematized interpretation of life and its problems. Perhaps it is nothing but a sort of optimism, based on feeling rather than on thought, and willing to accept any degree of undesirability imputed to life as it stands revealed to us for the moment. It is a belief in the future rather than in the present, a hope placed in coming generations rather than in those now occupying the world. It implies a trust in the power of man to wrest a final, satisfactory meaning out of even the most paradoxical and menacing aspects of human existence. It is a faith filled with humility and free from all fatuity. It is the faith which I believe will be forged by this century out of pangs and qualms and dread experiences compared with which all the sufferings of past ages must appear like those imagined sorrows that haunt man's infancy without ever seriously detracting from its bright dawn. And I believe that the United States will do more than any other country toward the shaping of this new faith, which will equally inspire its dreamers and its practical men. But because he dares not trust himself to it, even in moments when its glory seems to hover over his hyper-sensitive soul, Herrick, although so much both of American and artist, does not seem to be the man whom it will be granted to bring the new day and the new race to ultimate self-revelation. For this failure on his part, life has to be blamed, and not he, as it is temperamental and wholly unrelated to willed effort of any kind.

I can still recall how the reading of Herrick's earlier works, undertaken almost in the order of their appearance, thrilled me with a sense of continued, consistent growth. In "The Gospel of Freedom" I found him still groping and rather thin as to contents. But with "The Web of Life" he seemed to have discovered himself both in regard to manner and matter. Thence he pushed steadily onward until a climax was reached in "Together." This book is to me the supreme embodiment of the essential Herrick. As we see him there, he appears observant, tolerant and broadly interested in life's fundamental realities; but also a little too materialistic and sceptical, and for this reason somewhat inconclusive. To my mind "Together" will always remain one of the crowning glories of a thoroughly indigenous naturalism, which nevertheless shows plainly the fruitful inheritance of Dickens and Thackeray, the moral impetus obtained from the Russians, and the sobering influence of the great French novelists from Balzac to Maupassant.

While reading "Together," I felt that only one more step would be needed to make its author one of the world's enduring story tellers. But I felt also that this step, if effective, could imply nothing less than the passing of boundaries inherent in the writer's own nature. The taking of this one additional step would, I felt, mean the accomplishment of the seemingly impossible. Yet my first impression was, when "A Life for a Life" appeared, that such a step had actually been taken. Later I realized that, while an effort of remarkable intensity had been made by the author to outstrip his own inherent conditionings, the effort had been, on the whole, unsuccessful. But the very shortcomings of the book seemed still to promise a conscious and lasting rise to levels theretofore visited only in rare moments. The novel was vaguer in design and spirit than its predecessors, and it was less balanced in expression, but it was also braver and warmer and more human. Above all, it held so much more of that natural symbolism without which thought must always tend toward ultimate sterility. For once Herrick had tried as he knew best to surrender himself and his art to a mysticism that had now and then furnished a noticeable undercurrent in some of his earlier work, but of which he had until then seemed a little ashamed and distinctly afraid.

The leopard had all but changed its spots. But the very limitations which made for success up to a certain point, while they were accepted, had proved fatal in this case of their attempted defiance. Though this caused me some misgivings at the time, I clung to my hopes on behalf of Herrick's future until I had read "The Healer." Then I bowed my head to what began to seem inevitable. In doing so, I may have been premature, seeing that Herrick is still in his forties. But the book marks more than a retrogression: it has the depressing aspect of being written to glorify not only the author's inherent restrictions, but the reflection cast by these upon the surrounding world. It is the book of a man who has grown tired of aiming at the unattainable, and who for this reason seems inclined to quarrel with whomsoever might demand such aspirations of him. It is an apotheosis of spiritual faintheartedness, one might say, with not a trace left of any straining toward those sunlit heights that were so nearly reached in the previous book. But just on this account it is a very human work, startlingly personal in its revelation of the author's instinctive reactions and innermost disbeliefs.

The central figure, which has given the novel its name, is a man possessed of an unusual gift, who has fled into the wilderness to redeem that gift from certain habits fatal to its exercise. In his refuge he is overtaken by destiny shaped as a young woman whose life is trembling in the balance. Her extreme need serves to reveal the unclouding of his gift. Other demands on it are met with increasing self-confidence and no thought of reward. Even in the wilderness, however, such feats suffice to create a reputation. The distant world of sophistications and artificialities hears of the man and wants to capture him for its own mean uses. For a time he holds it at bay. But love has bound him to the woman whose life he once saved, and she has come straight out of the world he scorns and fears. This world she has left for him, and with him she accepts the wilderness until the child arrives. Then the chain never quite dropped by the young mother is pulled in link by link. And through her the man is caught also. Before he knows what has happened to him, he is selling his gift for money, with the final result that it deserts him once more, and now for ever. A catastrophe sweeps away the spot where the memory of earlier freedom had helped to keep him captive, and he avails himself of this opportunity to flee into another wilderness—that of a crowded, sordid city slum. His gift is gone, but his skill remains, and to the latter he adds a growing comprehension of what is required by such a gift as had been his. Armed with this new light, he sets out to develop in others the gift lost for ever to himself.

If we brush aside minor details and ramifications, we find at the bottom of this story a triangular conflict reaching beyond the individual characters. In the final analysis it involves man and woman and the world in which they have to live. But the third of these factors, the world, has a double aspect, as civilization in general, and as the specialization of it which makes up a man's professional environment. With Herrick's criticism of either one of these aspects I have little fault to find, though it is frequently more onesided than the dramatic tension of the story demands. When dealing with the shortcomings of the medical profession in particular, he has been led to "commit himself," both in diagnosis and remedial suggestions, to an extent quite uncommon to him. There is not the least doubt in his mind that the poison paralyzing the noblest activity of that profession is its increasing commercialization—that, under existing conditions, it is hopelessly cursed by "the base bargain of money for life." Speaking of the vast uninspired membership he says that "they are exploiting the human body and the human soul for private profit." And the one remedy he can suggest against this "prostitution" of the physician's calling is that "all medicine, all attempt at healing, should be institutionalized," so that "medical service should be free for all, provided by society as a whole for its own preservation and betterment." It is the remedy recommended by Bernard Shaw in his preface to "The Doctor's Dilemma," and one that is more and more coming to be considered inevitable by social students. From Shaw the proposition of such a remedy comes naturally as a part of his general acceptance of socialism as the one way out of our present evil state. From Herrick it comes as a sign of rare self-conquest, for his instinctive tendency would be to draw back from anything connected with an "ism" as from contagion.

Hardly less bitter, but a great deal less precise, is Herrick's arraignment of the part played by civilization in its entirety as a retarding medium through which genius literally has to fight its way toward some sort of fulfillment that is sure to fall short of its inherent possibilities. Of course, every one knows that almost all human institutions and most human beings are expressly designed to delay the process of change which in retrospect is seen as progress. But on the part played by all such resistance as a selective principle Herrick has bestowed small, if any, attention. And in this connection he gives one of the most typical illustrations of what I have called his "spiritual faintheartedness." Strindberg's eager acceptance of conflict as life's main attraction is wholly foreign to him. He bewails the conflict between genius and the world not only because it is distasteful to him in itself, but because he seems to look upon the rightness of it as resting wholly with one of the parties to it.

Whether pitched against woman directly, or against the civilization of which, in Herrick's view, she is the sole creator, man has the right on his side, and his justification springs from his mission as life's agent of perfective development. There is truth back of this view, but it is too onesided by far, and it shows a lack of penetration—or perhaps of the courage needed to realize that progress is gradual and devious, so that often the enforced compromise which at first glance appears like a surrender of all ideals may, on closer scrutiny, reveal itself as a means for the firmer establishment or more effective embodiment of those very ideals. And in his regrets at the enslavement of genius by economical necessities, Herrick fails to question how many of the world's masterpieces would have remained uncreated if no external factor had pressed upon their creators that compromise which, unfortunately, remains inseparable from every outward materialization of an inward vision. It is with strange feelings, indeed, that I notice how nearly identical Herrick's attitude on this particular point is with the orthodox Marxian socialist's outcry against any proposition to give him less than all he wants.

Where Herrick fails most strikingly, however, and most saddeningly, is in his view on woman and her relation to man's experimental proclivities. As seen by him, the civilization she is charged with having made does not mean order placed in complementary juxtaposition to progress, but only material comfort opposed to spiritual freedom. The falseness of this view does not depend so much on the part he assigns to woman, as on his failure to grasp the ultimate purpose of that part as well as the fact that she is playing it not by choice, but under the compelling direction of life itself. He sees that she likes to "shop," that she is emotional to the verge of sentimentality, and that she is prone to turn her look backwards. That her "shopping" may be a modern equivalent for her more primitive tendency to collect and produce useful things, he does not see—or he disregards such an interpretation, if it has occurred to him. All that he does is to contrast the qualities just mentioned with man's forward glance and predominant intellectuality —and out of mere difference he draws an excuse for condemnation so sweeping that it precludes any serious attempt to comprehend and explain. That, if she were what he wants her to be rather than what she is, woman might fail in the mission assigned to her by life as the human factor making for order and concreteness, seems almost unthinkable to him.

Yet he is not as blind as he permits himself to appear at times. All his women are not soft things, bent above all on cuddling in front of a luxurious fireside. One of them has the hardihood to assert that "the time will come when single women like me, who work as men work, will have the courage to love and bear children if they need to—and men will respect them." Another one, own daughter to the Healer himself, is quite masculine in her contempt for the softer side of life, and also in her passion for perfective achievement. And the author, speaking in his own person, is forced to admit that "the world has slowly struggled forth from the squaw era, and must perforce accord more and ever more rights to these bearers of the sacred seed, however unfitted they may be at present for their liberty and self-direction." He sees that the old is dead, but he dares not hail the new as king. He sees the truth, however vaguely, but he dares not draw the right conclusions from it. It means, I think, that Herrick is emotionally conservative and cannot but hate the necessity for movement occasioned by his intellectual recognition of serious shortcomings in our present social organization. There is a pitched battle ever raging between his vision, which tells him we cannot stay where we are, and his feelings, which recoil from the unknown, and so it is but natural that he should land in pessimistic resignation as the one way of bearing life. But resignation without a constructive purpose back of it is the last thing that could appeal to the spirit of this new-born century.

W. B. Yeats has furnished me with an excellent illustration of the possibility to observe in woman all that Herrick has seen, without being similarly frightened or repelled by it. "Strange paradox of the woman nature," Herrick cries in one place: "to seek the normal and sigh for the supernal, to lap herself in comfort and dream of the stars." But Yeats, having the self-same facts in mind, is merely moved to speak smilingly of "woman, who, perhaps because she is wholly conventional herself, loves the unexpected, the crooked, the bewildering." In one sense these two passages are identical; in another sense they are antithetical. For when Herrick stops with an accusation, Yeats goes on to an explanation. And the basis of it is just that conception of all being as a seemingly destructive, but actually constructive, interaction between complementary opposites, which I regard as one of the main keys to life's many riddles. But to perceive universal existence in this light is impossible without faith, and once more I must repeat that faith is just what Herrick lacks—or, to be more exact, he lacks the spiritual courage needed to accept a faith that in the end might prove a delusion.

On this fact, did it pertain only to Herrick himself, I should not harp with such insistency. But I have long ago indicated the extent to which I hold his case typical, when I named my earlier study of his work "The Americanism of Robert Herrick." Then I used the word "Americanism" in a wholly approving sense. Now I feel compelled to use it more ambiguously. For it is in his faults no less than in his merits, in his inhibitions no less than in his impulses, that Herrick appears to me one of the most national of our living writers. There are two currents at work within this people: one emotional and idealistic; the other sceptical and materialistic. The manifestations of the former current range all the way from such Utopian dreams as the Brook Farm experiment to such practical efforts for betterment as the progressive movement of the last few years. The second current has given us men like Mark Twain and Charles A. Dana, but it has also made possible such organizations as our various local or national "machines." The idealistic current is the natural expression of a young, healthy, and on the whole happy nation when it turns into itself for light and inspiration. The sceptical current results from such a nation's comparison of itself with more sophisticated human aggregates; and while it is no less needful than the other one, its immediate product is often a fear on the part of the young and still somewhat uncouth nation to "be itself." On the other side of the ocean the outcome of this fear is often spoken of as "American cynicism," and not entirely without warrant. For just this kind of excessive dread at being "taken in" is what leads so easily—in men as in nations—to a quick sneer at anything and everything which may possibly serve as a trap.

It is, after all, strange to find such a tendency operative in a man of Herrick's calibre and character. Some might hasten to ascribe it to his life-long academical environment, but I need only mention a few names, like those of William James, William Vaughan Moody and William Lyon Phelps, for instance, to invalidate any such conclusions in advance. The weakness—if weakness it be, as I have dared to assume—may prove innate and irresistible, as "The Healer" has caused me to fear. But it is also possible, in spite of all I have said so far, that it may prove, to some extent at least, the momentarily exaggerated result of influences that will disappear after a while. And I am as anxious as ever to hope that this will prove the case. The years through which Herrick has been passing—those of the middle forties—are almost invariably critical in the lives of largely gifted men. And I feel practically certain that some sort of mental crisis has cooperated in making "The Healer" what it is. If I be right in this, then the issue must remain in doubt until the crisis is ended. Thus I am led to conclude in a vein of optimism that may seem contradictory of what I have said before, but as it places me on the hopeful side of the problem involved, I do not regret it.

THE GREATER EDITH WHARTON

THE Berkshire region, with the northwestern part of Connecticut counted in, is one of the most attractive in the country. Its rolling, forest-clad hills and willow-screened valley nooks, its sheltered lakelets and meandering rivers, draw seekers of peace and of pleasure from all the Eastern money centres. These visitors speak glowingly of the early summer's pale serenity, of the fall's rapturous color riot, of glittering, almost graspable harvest moons, and of white, fleecy clouds sailing the tender blue of the sky from one sombrely smiling hilltop to another.

Yet this is a tragic country—tragic because of what it has done to the men choosing it for their home. In spite of that very beauty by which it tempted and trapped the first settlers, it is essentially a barren country, made for show rather than for use. In desperate struggle with its cutting winds, its snow-smothered winters, and its stony soil, one of the bravest populations any land could boast has slowly gone down to defeat and destruction. It is a death-doomed people, drained of its vitality by disease and emigration, rendered anemic and lethargic by the harshness of its lot, and withered as a branch severed from the trunk.

This is the country which Mrs. Wharton has chosen as setting for one of her recent novels, "Ethan Frome." And as we look at it with the keen vision that is hers, the ancient spinners of fate become transformed into those modern Norns whom we have named Climate, Soil and Race. The thread of events used by Mrs. Wharton for her purpose is of the slimmest and simplest. Ethan Frome is the last sprout of a characteristic Berkshire family. At twenty-eight he has been worn down to the resignation of an old man. He has seen first one and then the other of his parents yield up reason and life under the blows of a fate that must be held logical rather than unkind. He has seen the inherited hillside farm run dry as an old cow. Panic-stricken by the hemming solitude, he has clutched at the one human being that ever showed a willingness to share his fate; and thus he has become saddled with a wife seven years his senior—a dyspeptic, self-centred, unlovable being with a genius for imaginary invalidism and a passion for patent medicines. Into this blighted and blighting home comes a young girl with a pretty face and a soft heart—not an extraordinary girl, but one whose main charm lies in a desire to give and get sympathy not uncommon in youth when sundered from all its natural ties.

Love steals into the hearts of these two. And at the same time the older woman's heart grows increasingly heavy with a jealousy that is not rendered less bitter by its failure of open expression. Step by step, yet within a brief space and without introduction of a single useless detail, the author reveals love and jealousy growing apace, until at last the fatal moment of open clash can no longer be avoided. The girl is sent away by the wife. Ethan plans to go with his love toward a new life in the West. This plan is checked not by any conscientious scruples, but by poverty—by actual inability to raise the small sum needed for travelling expenses.

Spurred into undisguised defiance, he insists on driving the young girl down to the railroad station in person. At the moment of separation utter despair floods their hearts. They are standing at the top of the snow-carpeted hill down which they had hoped to go coasting together some moonlit evening. There is a sled left behind by departed merry-makers. The course is made dangerous by a big elm standing too close to its most difficult turn. Down the glassy smoothness of that hill the two lovers glide together in search not of pleasure but of a common death. And under the firm pressure of Ethan's heel, the sled speeds straight into the menacing tree trunk.

Few features of this remarkable book stand out more strikingly than its general design, by which the author has managed to satisfy at once our craving for surprise and our dislike of too much surprise. From the very start the shadow of that final "smash-up" lies over the pages of the book. We know that everything else must lead up to it. We know that Ethan himself is to come out of it as a man crippled and cursed forever afterward. And we know also that he must return to Zeena, the wife, and that the ruinous purchases of quack remedies will go on as before. But what of the second traveller on that sled speeding toward the consummation so often denied to the few that seek it? What of Matt? Not a word is said in advance as to her fate.

And so, when the teller of the story, the young engineer from the outside, having discovered and told all the rest, at last by a conspiracy of circumstances finds his way

EDITH WHARTON

into Ethan's home—otherwise closed to all the world but the owner—the shock of what the visitor discovers there leaves an impression on the reader's mind rarely equalled in the annals of fiction. For there, in the bare, inhospitable kitchen, where Zeena once brooded over her jealousy and Matt huddled her love—there the visitor meets both of them alive. Matt as a peevish, helpless, narrow-featured invalid with a broken back, and Zeena as a resigned, dull-hearted nurse. And there Ethan has to live the rest of his spoiled life between those two spectres of his lost hopes: the woman he needed and the woman he loved. All other tragedies that I can think of seem mild and bearable beside this one. What is death, or sorrowing for the dead, in comparison with a life chained to the dead remains of what might have been love?

Even to a mere reader such an outcome might seem unendurable—not to be born in mere print, as a tale told rather than an experienced fact—but for one consideration. And this one redeeming factor asserts itself subtly throughout the book, though Mrs. Wharton never refers to it in plain words. It is this: that, after all, the tragedy unveiled to us is social rather than personal. It is so overwhelming that the modern mind rebels against it as a typical specimen of human experience. And if it had no social side, if it implied only what it brought of suffering and sorrow to the partakers in it, then we could do little but cry out in self-protective impatience: "Sweep off the shambles and let us pass on!" As it is, and because that social aspect asserts itself so irresistibly, we are led into almost overlooking what those crushed lives must have meant to those living them.

Ethan and Matt and Zeena are, indeed, as real as men and women can become in a book. But just because we see them thus, and because their common fate is so insufferably pitiful, that process of mental cauterization by which life guards itself against too rude shocks sets in even while we are reading. Just as we could not live on if we were not mercifully permitted to forget certain pains that have shot across our own fields of consciousness, so we are here instinctively moved to "shake off" the thought of Ethan and Matt and Zeena as individual sufferers. They become instead embodiments of large groups and whole strata; and the dominant thought left behind by the book is not concerned with the awfulness of human existence, but with the social loss involved in such wasting of human lives.

"Ethan Frome" is to me above all else a judgment on that system which fails to redeem such villages as Mrs. Wharton's Starkfield. And I am not now preaching socialism in the narrower sense. I am talking it in a sense in which it is being more and more accepted by those most fervently bent on orderly progress. I am pleading merely for the extension of certain forms of social cooperation and coordination—or call it simply organization—that have already been found inevitable in many fields of human activity. If a little crew of wrecked sailors be cast up on some coral reef in midocean, we do not say that they deserve their fate, nor do we demand that they rely wholly on their own resources for escape. The moment we learn of their plight, we send a vessel to relieve them. And this we do not only for their sake but for our own—because we need those men to carry on the world's business, and because we do not want to discourage other men from engaging in their perilous trade.

Those who dwell in our thousand and one Starkfields are just such wrecked mariners, fallen into their hapless positions by no fault of their own. And though helpless now, they need by no means prove useless under different conditions. Vessels should be sent to take them off their barren hillsides—or social effort should be employed in making those hillsides fruitful once more. There is hardly an inch of

EDITH WHARTON

ground that has not its use of some kind—its paying use. There is hardly a human being, either, who cannot be rendered socially paying if given a chance. This we must learn ere the new day can be hoped for.

Mrs. Wharton has wisely refrained from every attempt at pointing toward a solving way. All she has done—and all she was called on to do—was to reveal the presence of Starkfield and its population of Fromes within a social body that should contain nothing but living and growing tissue. In doing this, and doing it with her usual exquisiteness of word and phrase and portraiture, Mrs. Wharton has passed from individual to social art; from the art that excites to that which incites.

Glancing over the all too brief volume in retrospect, I can find only one point where it suggests a certain degree of failure, of growth still unachieved. With the building of the tale as it now stands I can have no fault to find. It is against a certain lack of outlook, a certain onesidedness of conception, that I direct my adverse criticism. And to what I say along this line, the author may, of course, reply that what I am wishing for did not fall within the scope of her plan. And yet I wish it had!

Let me try to explain, though the task undoubtedly will prove hard—and let me be frankly personal in order to be wholly just. As I read the book now, I come away with an impression that, in the author's mind at least, the one thing needed to change Ethan's life from a hell to a heaven would have been the full and free expression of his love for Matt. Had Zeena died and Matt married him, then, I am made to feel, the barren farm of Ethan might have blossomed once more; the strangled dreams of his youth might have ceased to harass and haunt his soul; nay, life in its entirety might have changed its face.

This is the very thing which poets through the ages have been tempting man to believe. It is the very thing which I cannot accept as a true interpretation of life's reality. Love is not a cure-all capable of righting all wrongs in an ill-managed world. It is an appetite, if you please; or, if so it please you better, it is a spiritual force springing from one of life's most material aspects. But at any rate it is a necessity—one of several—and as such it is bound to work havoc when not filled. But if, on the other hand, it be properly satisfied, then it reveals itself promptly as no end in itself, but a means to other ends—a prerequisite to the filling of new and no less essential necessities. We need love to live properly, but we can no more live properly on love alone than we can do so on bread.

Romantic love, as idealized for us by our sentimental-minded forefathers, has long ago gone into bankruptcy. Henrik Ibsen sat as judge in the case, and George Bernard Shaw was appointed receiver with full power to reorganize the failing concern. And so it is becoming more evident with every passing day that the race of pale youths and slender-waisted maidens who took or lost their own lives because of "unrequited love" never really belonged to this world.

Of course, if you have no soul-dominating interest to focus your activities, and you happen to pick up such an interest in the shape of a love dream, however silly or commonplace, and fate wakes you prematurely out of your sweet dream, then you are very likely to sink back into something much worse than your previous state of comparatively harmless inanition. But if, on the other hand, all your faculties are normally employed; if each day brings you new problems to solve, and if life does not deny you every means of applying your solutions, then the same kind of love dream, ending in pretty much the same way, may change but not mar the rest of your life. It will then serve as an added impetus toward activities already dear to your heart. The law of compensation will assert itself— energy will be transmitted instead of wasted

—and life will go on even more effectively, though perhaps less placidly than before.

Had Zeena died and Matt married Ethan—well, it is my private belief that inside of a few years life on that farm would have been practically what it was before Matt arrived, with Matt playing the part of a Zeena II—different, of course, and yet the same. For the life in our Starkfields is cursed or saved not by this or that single incident, not by the presence or absence of this or that individual. "Most smart ones get away," says the old stage driver in Mrs. Wharton's book. The curse lies in staying there, in breathing the crushing, choking atmosphere of Starkfieldian sterility.

Ethan was doomed when he did not get away as a boy. Having returned and stayed for a certain length of time, his life was no longer susceptible to more than momentary alleviation. And a forewarning of this fact I read out of Mrs. Wharton's repeated references to Matt's physical frailty—a state of mind and body certain to have made her an easy victim of the Starkfield atmosphere even if no "smash-up" had been the cause of her stay within it. A few weeks or months of complete surrender to love's bliss would to Ethan have been what the grog is to the fainting stoker in the ocean steamer's boiler-room. That grog may bring temporary relief, it may save life, and it may even carry with it a quick sting of pleasure, but it cannot turn stoking into a wholesome or pleasurable task. And life in a place untouched by the onward sweep of the world, especially when lived by individuals soured and weakened by a too long and too hard struggle against conditions unfit for any human being, is nothing but another form of stoking. For saying which each present Starkfield inhabitant will probably rise up and curse the rash critic.

MAN'S BEGINNING AND END

OF course, the *how* as well as the *when* of man's first emergence out of brute animality lies hidden in the mists of primal day. And no more do we know at what time or under what circumstances humanity as a whole may pass out of being. But every so often science makes a guess at both problems—than which there are few more tempting to the human mind—and where the scientist's scales and figures fail, there the poet's fancy steps in and completes what by the former was barely suggested. Contributing to these flights of fancy, a Danish novelist and a Russian playwright have undertaken to portray the beginning and the end of man.

Basing their far-reaching dreams on the very last words of modern physics, biology and sociology, these two European writers have audaciously ventured into the paths once trod so gloriously by John of Patmos and Milton. The novelist is Johannes V. Jensen, whose sound learning and vivid narrative powers have assured his books a vogue far beyond the borders of his native country. The dramatist is Valerius Brjussoff, whose sombre, yet always noble and never morbid, genius has won him recognition in Germany at least, though his name here is practically unknown.

In a novel named "The Glacier," Jensen has tried to picture how man first became man in the true sense of the word—and the dominant idea of his book is that not pleasant ease, but struggle under the hardest kind of necessity was what finally raised man above the brute plane on which he probably dwelt while the northern parts of the globe were still covered with tropical vegetation and knew only one season— eternal summer.

The play by Brjussoff that balances and complements Jensen's novel is named

BEGINNING AND END 307

"Earth Wreck" and pictures dramatically the closing scenes in mankind's long and glorious career—scenes that by a last flaring up of human courage and human genius are turned from ignominious decay into tragical catastrophe.

In thus surveying man's earliest and last days within the span of two small volumes, one is struck by the presence of certain common ideas, although these ideas may figure quite differently in the drama and in the novel. Tools made by man play a conspicuous part in the Danish work, but there we see them slowly and painfully emerging under the pressure of immediate need. Just because they are so poor, so tentative, so hardly won, man is their master.

On the other hand, the background against which "Earth Wreck" is painted is a conquest of material nature so complete that the machinery by which man's existence is sustained seems to work almost without the aid of its creator. It had been started when man stood at the very apex of his power; it runs on when we see him in his hour of final decline—and we feel that it will go on moving long after the last man has drawn his last breath of vanishing air. And just because of its perfection, this machinery seems to rule man rather than to be ruled by him.

Still more interesting become the points of contact between the novel and the play if we turn from the physical to the spiritual plane. As in the opening chapters of "The Glacier" we behold the semi-human group out of which the symbolical first man emerged, we find the most characteristic trait of its members to be thoughtlessness—a certain aimless drifting whither the winds of heaven and the moods of the moment happen to tend. Again, turning to the play, we see and hear anemic men and women loll and chatter and drift, knowing nothing of a set purpose or of a will put through in face of a hostile universe. Man, ere he became man, was a child, and a child he must become once more ere he die his

BEGINNING AND END 309

final death, these two dreamers seem to say in unconscious unison.

Together with a steadily growing number of scientists, historians, and philosophers, Jensen believes that the cradle of civilized mankind—which to him means the Aryan races—stood in or near the so-called Baltic basin, probably in the middle and southern parts of Sweden. But in the catastrophe embraced in what is generally named the Glacial Period—the covering of all Northern Europe with a deep mat of ice and snow—he sees not a hindrance to mankind's further development, but its true beginning. Until then, during the Tertiary Period, the continent in question possessed the flora and fauna now shown by the equatorial regions—with this difference, however, that it was even more luxurious and varied, while showing less of that death-in-life, that strange flourishing of life right in the midst of decay, which is now so typical of our tropics. In those days European man lived from hand to mouth, picking his food as he went along and having no reason to develop forethought or purpose. And because such thought as he had was not projective—because it did not lead him to steadfast pursuit of a goal seen far in the distance—it could hardly be called thought at all.

Then began that change which altered the surface of the whole northern hemisphere—and perhaps the history of the entire globe. Where perennial sunshine had reigned, where evenly tempered heat had made all life thrive beyond any dreams of ours, there clouds began to hide the blue of the sky, the earth became wrapt in gloom, rain poured forth as if to deluge whatever there was of life, and the stated rotation of the seasons began—but began with what was practically the substitution of everlasting winter for endless summer.

Primitive man suffered, but did not reason about his sufferings. Step by step he fell back before the oncoming Arctic winter. League by league he yielded up the ground

BEGINNING AND END 311

that he should ever afterward recall as the Eden of his primal period. The introduction to "The Glacier" shows us the rear-guard of such a retreating horde. In this rear-guard, however, there is one man who differs from the rest. His name is Dreng—which is only the old Norse name for "young man." He belongs to the favored family, whose duty and privilege it is to tend the sacred fire—the fire which the legendary ancestor of that family was said to have snatched from the edge of the volcano. If this fire be extinguished there is no way of relighting it.

At night, while the rest of the little band sleeps, Dreng guards and feeds the fire. The rain is falling all around him. The virginal forest is astir with sounds not only of the northern wind that is breaking its trees, but of wild beasts on the march toward milder climes. The life of that part of the continent is doomed. Some of the wild creatures—most of them—flee before the cold and are saved. A few, like the sabre-toothed tiger and the cave lion, stay and perish.

The difference between Dreng and the rest is that he remembers where the others forget; that he inclines to resist where they incline to yield. At the fire he is shaping his rude flint weapon, and that, too, stirs dreams in his crude mind—dreams of a weapon better than anybody has ever seen. In other words, Dreng is a natural freak; he represents one of those leaps which nature now and then takes into the future —we call them by the name of genius nowadays.

To Dreng, sitting there at the fire, listening to the roar of the wind and the tramp of the beasts, it seems that some person, some being like himself, some unseen enemy, must be behind the changes that are forcing them farther and farther away from the homes once occupied in such happy unconcern. And his dawning thought leads him to go in search for that enemy.

Preparing the fire so that it will last

BEGINNING AND END 313

until his return, he deserts his trusted post and leaves his sleeping, childlike comrades. Through the flooded forest, up the sides of the nearest hills he makes his slow way. For the first time he meets snow and ice. Everywhere he beholds disaster—but the being that causes the disaster cannot be found. He returns, finds the fire gone, the troupe vanished. And when he overtakes them he is stoned back as a traitor, an enemy.

Made an outcast, Dreng turns northward. There is more anger than sorrow in his wildly stirring heart. And under the pressure of the mood, moved perhaps by his destiny, he starts straight into the heart of the winter. Hardship after hardship, one worse than the other, marks his aimless way. But he is still young, a giant of build, and with that strange new fire within that is to break into the full flame of a purposive will by and by. As Jensen pictures him, he resembles closely the reconstructed Neanderthal man—with craggy brows and protruding jaws, with arms reaching to the knees and hair covering every part of the body, but for all that an animal that no longer walks on all fours.

Half-dead with cold, Dreng breaks into the hole of a hibernating bear. A battle of life and death follows between the intruder and the aroused Bruin. Dreng, armed with his trusty stone axe—his sole weapon, so far—conquers, but not until he has lost one eye. For throughout his book, Jensen has connected the story with the old myths, and Dreng is Odin, Wotan, the First Father, the One-Eyed. And like Wotan, Dreng buys knowledge by the loss of his eye—the knowledge of clothes. For having slain the bear, and supped off his warm blood, he is driven by the cold to cut open the carcass and crawl into it for protection.

The next step is to flay off the skin and wrap it around the body. Then he bethinks himself of tying the bear's dangling paws under his own feet, so as to keep them from

BEGINNING AND END

being cut by the ice—and he has shoes. He learns to wrap the hides of smaller beasts about his legs, and to cut out narrow strips with which to tie them into place. He is clothed.

As he lives thus, in lonely pursuit of whatever life is left on the icefields, two things stand out above all others and grave themselves on his consciousness. One is the ever-growing glacier which has taken the place of what was once the Scandinavian peninsula, and will be so once more in the fullness of time. The other one is the mammoth—the pachyderm that refused to yield before the cold, and that has now become the king of the icy wastes.

In the north there is always the bright green glare of the glacier's advancing ice wall. And against the deep, blinking winter sky the titanic bulk of the mammoth is ever so often caught in monstrous silhouette, swaying slowly back and forth, the very embodiment of self-sufficient loneliness.

When the brief and wet summer comes, the birds and beasts seek back toward the old homes. The birds succeed, and establish those habits of migration that still last. The crawling and running things on the ground try in vain, and have to turn back—or if they push on, it is only to perish.

In the meantime Dreng has acquired his first companion—a stray member of a pack of dogs that has shadowed his steps and shared his hunting. This one seems, like Dreng himself, to possess some spark brighter than any burning within the crania of the rest. From merely following the man's hunt he learns to take part in it, to do his share—but still only on sufferance. Between man and dog there is at first nothing but an armed truce, but gradually this grows into actual companionship and cooperation.

Now and then the heart of Dreng is vaguely haunted by a craving for other men, and in the summertime he manages now and then to get far enough southward

BEGINNING AND END

to find some creatures like himself. But when he overtakes them they are just so much prey, and—he eats them. Once, however, he hunts such a prey—one that looks different from the rest—and overtakes it only after a three days' pursuit. It is a woman. They meet on the shores of the ocean. And there the first monogamistic marriage begins. Moa she is called when the first children have come and given her a name. She returns with Dreng to the glacier, and from that moment the beginning of civilized humanity may be counted.

As hunting and slaying is the main instinct of Dreng—besides making weapons for the hunt—so picking up things is the principal characteristic of Moa. By merely storing things out of curiosity or from some instinct like that moving rooks and crows, she learns to use grains and roots and fruits.

The man's symbol is the axe. Hers is the basket. He makes his clothes out of hides as before and strings them together with strips of chewed hide. She gathers mammoth wool from the dwarf firs and weaves it crudely into a fabric more suitable to her nature. They live in caves or behind shelters rudely put together of rocks piled on each other. During the long winters dried meat and dried roots form their only food.

But in the mind of Dreng lies the memory of the fire he used to guard. As the winters grow worse and worse, the prey scarce and scarcer, he seems almost seized with a mania to find that fire. There is one clue—the tiny sparks flying from the flints when he shapes his weapons. And one winter, the worst of all, he simply spends his time hammering stone after stone and dreaming that out of some of them the fire may come. And finally it comes. For he has happened to find a piece of iron ore at last, and as it strikes against the flint, sparks of a different kind—big, burning sparks—are scattered in every direction.

The picture of Dreng dancing around the first fire really made by man and the visions

BEGINNING AND END

seen by him in the following night, when he is too excited to sleep, form some of the best parts of this notable volume. But when Dreng begins to dance, Moa rushes in fright out of the rock house, and there she stands with inward-turned toes, staring in mixed surprise and pleasure, but on the whole finding everything quite natural. "Her man, her god, had chosen to make the fire, and that was only to be expected, for what could he not do?"

On the rocky island, in the midst of the glacier, where Dreng and Moa had found a refuge, there the sons and daughters of that first couple remain and increase. They do just what Dreng and Moa used to do. The descendants in a straight line of Dreng's eldest son are guardians of the fire stone, and as such they take toll from the rest, being at once chieftains and medicine men. And very few changes occur, although they learn to keep reindeer for the sake of the milk.

Thousands of years pass along. There

has been another subtle change in the seasons. The winters are growing shorter, the summers longer and hotter. The rock island is overcrowded, and the privileged family is becoming more arrogant. Thus things conspire to produce another outcast, the second Dreng—Whitebear named—who is to take mankind away from the glacier and back to the regions where the ice is already melting away. In this second leader we have the figure of Thor, the god of skill and of fertility. He and his wife, Vaar (Spring), settle down near where stands now Stockholm, and from there, through adventures that must be passed over here, a new start is made, the start that has given us the nations that rule the western world to-day.

Whitebear, who builds the first ship and makes the first wagon, leads us logically up to that state of material perfection which we encounter in Brjussoff's play. How many millenniums from those first stumbling but fateful steps of Dreng to the opening scene

BEGINNING AND END 321

in "Earth Wreck," in the gorgeous, mystical Hall of the Blue Basin, who can tell? But that the line of development thus marked by its first and last stations is logical we can hardly doubt.

And we are made to understand that, through millennium after millennium, mankind grew and grew—in power and insight, in control of nature and of itself—until at last men had the whole earth in their hands as one immense tool. And at that supreme moment, with so much of the universe lying like an open book before them, the leaders of mankind saw that even a race like theirs must die. And they set out to postpone that fatal moment with all the miraculous skill at their command.

They, too, have felt an approaching change, just as did the contemporaries of Dreng. But this time it consists in a steady thinning out of the terrestrial atmosphere. And they foresee the day when there shall not be enough air left on the earth for any creature to live in. By that time the whole

322 VOICES OF TO-MORROW

surface of the earth is covered by men, living together in cooperation based on insight rather than on sentiment. To move them all as one body is possible and other creatures there are none to count with. Food is obtained artificially, and so the thought of making all life artificial except the breeding of new men comes quite easily to them.

Digging down and building up, they establish a kind of shell for the earth. There, in several stories, gloriously housed, mankind lives. Within that shell there is air enough, artificially made or renewed. Outside of it the atmosphere may disappear as fate has decreed it must; mankind will live on for all that. Water and light and food are produced by machines that take their motive power from the internal heat of the globe—machines so perfected that they practically run themselves. Thus the inevitable is postponed, but not disposed of.

Housed in that shell, with every material need carefully provided for, mankind begins

BEGINNING AND END

to atrophy, to wither. Births decrease, the race degenerates slowly without knowing it, and its numbers fall off. Thus perhaps thousands of years pass again—and probably nothing is more characteristic of those years than the slow but steady blunting of man's will, of his power of concentrated attention, of his capacity for dogged perseverance. The accumulated spiritual treasures are by decrees reduced to dead letters, until they are quite forgotten. Here and there only a sage with his circle of scholars maintains the old traditions, the old learning, the old ambitions on behalf of humanity as the crown and glory of universal creation.

And thus is forgotten at last even that knowledge of ruthless facts which caused men to coat the earth with its triple shell of human habitations. Beyond the roofs of their halls nobody looks. That there is no air outside those roofs only one living man knows. As their numbers decline, those that survive gravitate toward the lower halls, nearer the heart of that earth which sustains them. There, in a deep-dug central shaft, are the central power generators that run and regulate the entire material part of their existence. That is to them the centre of life—but they have long ceased to know how to control those machines, and when the play opens, no one then living has ever looked upon the sun.

A group of women lounging listlessly around the blue basin after which the hall is named—that is all we see in the beginning. There is no water in the basin. Other receptacles have thus gone dry, until each group has to wander through as many as twenty halls to get what they need of water. That once pipes actually led the life-giving fluid right into their private rooms, they do not even remember. And the light is also going out in hall after hall. Still there are enough habitable places left for the three millions of human creatures that represent the whole race.

The women talk without purpose—gossip, love, private troubles—just as to-day, but in a much more anemic fashion. The Sage—earth's oldest living man—comes with his scholars. And then there is an outcry. Somebody is brought in on the shoulders of his excited fellow-men. It is Newatl—the Dreng of the day. He has searched the old deserted halls and galleries. He has strayed on and on, moved by despairing realization of mankind's doom, until at last he has reached the uppermost story, and there—through a lofty window—he has beheld the paling stars and the rising sun.

Yes, the sun is still rising and setting, though men have not looked upon it for thousands of years. And now this man, who has seen the ever renewed, ever equally grand spectacle of the rising orb—this mankind's last genius—cries that he has found the way to a rejuvenated race. It is the old cry of "back to nature," but here uttered with a new meaning.

Others have seen and grasped the trend

of humanity's downward drift. Others have fretted their hearts out over it and sought for remedies, and principally a strange man named Teotl—for all the figures in this weird work bear names that bring our minds back to the old Aztecs of Mexico. Teotl is the head of the Order of the Liberator—a group of thirteen men and women who have made it their mission to bring mankind the one possible relief— death. Murder is their faith, and as one is caught at it and himself killed, a new recruit takes his place. Death is their god, and to death they sing hymns. He is the Liberator.

But the cry raised by Newatl breaks up the order. Once more the hope of life—of life in its old fullness and richness—is awakened. Newatl has recalled that there is a mechanism provided for the raising of the roofs that cover their halls. And what he proposes is to open those roofs, to let in the air—the air that is not there—and to restore to mankind the vigor that springs only from

BEGINNING AND END 327

a life in close contact with all the forces of nature.

The old Sage—Newatl's teacher—hears the cry, and in his heart it arouses quite another thought. He is the only one that still preserves the knowledge of what exists outside of their own shell. But instead of warning the others of what the raising of the roofs will mean, he decides that thus— by a catastrophe that has something lofty and noble in its suddenness and completeness—mankind will be saved from that complete relapse into primitive brutishness which he is foreseeing.

That is all. There is enough of action, of conflict between personalities, to make a real drama of it. But all this hardly concerns us here. Followed by Newatl, the man of the hour, and ten trusty scholars, the Sage penetrates to the deep-sunk rock chamber where the central power generators are located. Under his direction turns the cogged wheel that will raise the roofs from the uppermost halls. To those halls the crowd has repaired, eagerly awaiting the hour of rejuvenation, and there idly gossiping or as idly quarrelling about what is to be done, they meet their fate together.

It is a wonderful scene, that last one, where the sun breaks into the hall, and in its path comes death—not for one or a few, but for every living being within sight. Thus the Russian fancies the end of the race— brought about by what it still has of brain and heart, and rendered inevitable by the ruthlessly revolving cycles of evolution: from death to life and back to death again.